'92   C O

The Plan-Ahead Cookbook

THE
PLAN-AHEAD
COOKBOOK

300 Delectable Ways to Use Your Leftovers

By CEIL DYER

THE MACMILLAN COMPANY

The Macmillan Company
Collier-Macmillan Canada Ltd., Toronto, Ontario

Printed in the United States of America

Contents

Introduction

To BEGIN WITH, though making use of leftover food is almost as old as time—the first caveman soon learned to save yesterday's bone stew as sauce for tomorrow's rabbit—it can also be a method of cooking that is as new as tomorrow's computer and just as efficient.

It is as simple as this: by buying more than enough for a planned menu—that jumbo-size can of tomatoes for instance, a whole roast instead of those steaks, and that ten-pound bag of potatoes in place of a few loose ones—in other words, by buying in volume and in economy sizes, you will save money, and by *cooking* more than enough—preparing the makings for three, four, or even more meals at one "cooking"—you will save time. The results: better food for less effort and at lower cost, more interesting and imaginative menus, and, most important, more free hours for you to use as you like.

But does it really work? Of course it does, and not just now and again. This method of planned cooking has made life easier and more pleasant for me—as it can for you, each and every day of the week. To prove it, here's an example that starts with one of my own favorite Southern-style menus and ends with some really great made-from-leftovers food:

Baked Virginia Ham
with Pineapple
Candied Sweet Potatoes   **Crisp-cooked Broccoli**
Parker House Rolls
Fresh Strawberries with Homemade Sponge Cake
Coffee

A truly delicious meal, to my way of thinking, but, let's face it, not a quick one to bring to the table. Nonetheless, it's relatively easy, and look at the wealth of convenient leftover food it can provide if you plan. Here's just one of the ways it has worked for me in the past:

First, because I bought and baked the largest whole ham my oven would hold, I had enough left over for an elegant cold ham mousse to serve to Tuesday's bridge club, plus enough to make six ham sandwiches for a family midnight snack and also a dinner party main course, Louisiana ham and oyster jambalaya. In addition, because I cooked double the needed broccoli and three times the necessary amount of sweet potatoes, I had the makings for a broccoli soufflé and a sweet potato pie, this last a "quickie" made with already-in-the-freezer prepared pastry for crust. And, as if that were not enough, I also had two sponge cake layers to freeze for next week or next month.

What riches—and all made in less time than the telling. But, after all, not everyone likes ham, no matter how saving its ways. The point is that you can achieve the same results from almost any menu you plan.

In this rush-and-hurry world, what other method of cooking makes such downright good sense? None, I say, and I hope you agree, because not only will leftover cookery save "you" and your money, it can also make for the finest of true gourmet meals.

As students of *haute cuisine* well know, some of the best and most interesting recipes from Europe as well as both the Near and the Far East demand already cooked food as an ingredient of primary importance. These creations were never thought of as "second-time servings" by the good cooks who first made them. Each one is a masterpiece, a chef-d'oeuvre, and no matter how time-consuming, each is well worth making even if you have to start from scratch. With the "already cooked part" ready and waiting, however, these elegant dishes become, almost always, as quick and easy to make as ordinary hamburgers or bacon and eggs. Moreover, with today's modern refrigeration and ample freezer space, there is no reason why these makings cannot be on hand.

That rare and juicy center cut left from Sunday's roast can be wrapped and frozen, to reappear a month later in a superb beef Stroganoff. The accompanying leftover rice can be refrigerated in an airtight container, then used next week for a different and interesting, not to mention delicious, pilaf, and even those few leftover boiled carrots will make a light and airy soufflé for tomorrow or the day after if stored in a plastic bag. Indeed, if you are looking for ways to surprise and delight your family and friends at mealtime, leftovers can provide the answer and in a myriad of wonderful ways—and there, of course, is the reason for this book.

The recipes you will find here are all ones I have used many times. Some of them will undoubtedly be familiar to you, others both unusual and new. My versions do not take much effort, and I think they have a versatility you will enjoy. They can often be adapted to whatever ingredients are available at the moment, and I am sure you will do just this; however, the novice cook will find them both precise and accurate.

If you do not have sufficient leftover ingredients to prepare a particular dish, read on or browse through the index. You will find others to fit your need. You will also find ways to make use of "bits and pieces" at the beginning of many chapters as well as suggestions throughout the book for what to do with that "last little bit." You can make good use of any leftover food if you want to, and with a little imagination you will be amazed how good leftovers can be.

How exciting can you make *all* of the food that you cook? You can make it as exciting as you want. It's simply up to you—and I do hope this book will help.

Bon leftovers *appétit!*

Meat

Boiled Beef

CLASSIC BOILED BEEF—brisket, chuck, bottom round, rump, or cross rib—has always been high on the gourmet's list of "planned for second meal" cookery.

This rather bland, but delicious, meat is perfection when served cold with hot Dijon mustard, horseradish, pickles, or other piquant accompaniments.

If a hot dish is preferred, boiled beef may be reheated in its original cooking broth without loss of flavor, or this stock can be used as a base for rich gravy or sauce.

Stock, after fat is removed, may be reheated and served as clear soup, or it may be frozen, then put to good use many weeks later in any recipe that calls for brown stock.

TO STORE: Refrigerate covered, in cooking broth; use within one to two days. Or, wrap meat in moistureproof paper; refrigerate up to one week. Or, slice meat, wrap meal-size portions, in moistureproof paper, seal, and freeze; store in freezer up to three months.

BITS AND PIECES

Spread bite-size cubes of boiled beef with hot (Dijon-type) mustard. Top each cube with a small slice of crisp sweet pickle and spear with cocktail pick. Serve as hors d'oeuvre.

Spear bite-size cubes of boiled beef with cocktail picks. Serve as appetizers with well-seasoned tomato sauce and horseradish mixed half-and-half as a dip.

Cook fresh or frozen vegetables in beef broth, add diced boiled beef. Season with a bit of dry mustard.

Add diced boiled beef to potato salad or rice salad, or combine with equal parts chopped ripe tomato, bind with mayonnaise lightly seasoned with curry powder, and serve on crisp lettuce leaves.

Arrange overlapping thin slices of cold boiled beef on a long serving platter. Around them, place in alternate mounds thinly sliced cold boiled potatoes, cold boiled French-style green beans, quartered hard-cooked eggs, and tomato wedges. Sprinkle entire platter first with minced green onions, then with vinaigrette dressing (see page 225). Let stand at room temperature about one hour before serving. (This dish should be served cool but not chilled.) Garnish with sprigs of parsley just before serving.

BOEUF EN GELÉE
(Jellied Beef)

2 *tablespoons chopped celery*
2 *tablespoons chopped parsley*
1 *clove garlic, chopped*
1 *medium onion, stuck with one clove*
1 *bay leaf*
Dash of ground thyme
1 *teaspoon dried tarragon*

¼ *teaspoon salt*
3 *cups beef stock, from boiled beef (or see page 202)*
3 *envelopes unflavored gelatin*
3 *egg whites, lightly beaten*
½ *cup Madeira wine*
3 *cups finely diced cold boiled beef*

Combine all ingredients except wine and beef in large saucepan. Bring to boil, lower heat, and allow to simmer very gently for 20 to 25 minutes. Remove from heat and strain through a fine sieve lined with a triple thickness of cheesecloth which has been wrung out in cold water. Add Madeira. Refrigerate until mixture begins to thicken.

Add meat and pour into a lightly greased loaf pan. Refrigerate until firm.

Dip mold briefly in hot water. Unmold onto serving platter. Cut into slices and serve.

[6 *servings.*]

COLD BOILED BEEF WITH PEPPERS
AND ANCHOVY SAUCE

8 *to* 12 *¼-inch-thick slices of*
    cold boiled beef
3 *green peppers*
Water
2 *tablespoons olive oil*
1 *clove garlic*
2 *tablespoons minced green*
    onion

12 *to* 16 *anchovy fillets in oil,*
    minced but not drained
1 *tablespoon red wine vinegar*
Salt
½ *teaspoon coarsely ground*
    black pepper

Place cold beef slices on long serving platter. Let stand at
room temperature while preparing peppers and sauce.

Place peppers in large pot of water. Bring to full boil, remove from heat, let stand 10 minutes. Drain, peel off skins,
and cut into thin strips, discarding seed and fibers. Arrange
over meat in platter.

Heat oil with the garlic. Add green onion and anchovies,
including oil from can. Cook, stirring, over low heat about 2
minutes. Stir in vinegar, add salt and pepper.

Pour over green peppers and meat. Cool but do not over-
chill. Serve as buffet-supper dish or as antipasto.
[4 *servings.*]

BOILED BEEF À LA PROVENÇALE

4 *tablespoons butter*
½ *small clove garlic, minced*
3 *medium tomatoes, coarsely*
    chopped
1 *tablespoon tomato paste*
¼ *teaspoon salt*
½ *teaspoon freshly ground*
    black pepper

3 *medium onions, coarsely*
    chopped
2 *cups diced cold boiled beef*
Salt
Coarsely ground } *to taste*
    black pepper

Heat 2 tablespoons of the butter with the garlic in a small
saucepan. Add tomatoes and cook over moderate heat, chop-

ping the tomatoes still more as they cook, with the tip of a spatula. When this mixture has been reduced to a thick pulp, stir in the tomato paste, remove from heat, and season with salt and pepper. Set aside.

Heat the remaining butter in a large heavy skillet; add the onions and meat. Cook, stirring, until onions are limp, meat well heated. Stir in the tomato sauce and cook, stirring, a final minute. Correct seasoning with additional salt and pepper if desired. Serve over boiled rice or noodles.
[4 *servings.*]

BOILED BEEF SLICES IN HORSERADISH SAUCE

8 *to* 12 *slices cold boiled beef,*
  about ¼ *inch thick*
1 *tablespoon butter*
1 *tablespoon flour*
1 *cup beef stock, clear, without*
  fat

1 *cup light cream*
Salt ⎫
Pepper ⎬ *to taste*
2 *to* 3 *tablespoons grated*
  horseradish

Bring cold beef slices to room temperature.

Melt butter in large saucepan, stir in flour. When this is blended and bubbly, slowly stir in, first, beef stock, then cream. Cook over low heat without boiling, stirring frequently, until sauce begins to thicken. Add salt and pepper to taste, horseradish, and beef slices. Cook only until meat is well heated. Do not allow to boil. Serve with freshly cooked boiled potatoes and carrots.
[4 *servings.*]

CRISP COOKED VEGETABLES, BOILED BEEF, AND SOUR CREAM DRESSING

8 *to* 12 *slices of cold boiled beef, about* ¼ *inch thick*
2 *to* 3 *tablespoons vinaigrette dressing* (*see page* 225)

½ *cup mayonnaise*
½ *cup sour cream*
1 *teaspoon lemon juice*

6 *to* 8 *cups stock from boiled beef* (*fat removed*)
Salt, *if needed*
8 *small white onions, peeled*
4 *medium carrots, scraped and quartered*
1 *small cabbage, quartered, outer leaves removed*

Sprinkle cold beef slices with French dressing or vinaigrette sauce. Let stand at room temperature while preparing sauce—meat is best when served cool but not chilled.

Mix mayonnaise with sour cream and lemon juice. Place in serving dish or sauce boat. Refrigerate until ready to serve.

Bring stock to boil in large pot. Season with salt if necessary. Add onions. Cook over moderate heat for about 10 minutes. Add carrots; continue to cook only until vegetables are crisp-tender. Add cabbage and cook a final 3 to 5 minutes. (Cabbage especially should be crisp.) Drain vegetables, place around meat on platter in alternate groups. Serve sauce separately.

[4 *servings.*]

Roast Beef

THE MOST RESPECTED leftover meat in an American kitchen is very apt to be that carefully prepared, pink and juicy sirloin or rib roast. Too expensive to warrant waste, it is meticulously wrapped and stored. But to get full value for its high price, the same care must be taken for its reappearance at the table.

TO STORE: Wrap meat and bones in foil; refrigerate two to three days. Or, remove meat from bone, place in airtight container or wrap in moistureproof paper, and refrigerate up to one week. Or, remove meat from bone, slice or dice, wrap meal-size portions in moistureproof paper, seal edges; store in freezer two to three months. If meat has been removed from bones, wrap bones separately; refrigerate or freeze as above.

Refrigerate drippings or gravy separately; when gravy is well chilled, remove fat from surface. Cover container with foil or plastic wrap and seal edges, or place in airtight container. Refrigerate or freeze as above.

If rare beef is always your preference—and it usually is with the man of the house—undercook your roast; then, at first serving, carve a few slices first from one end, then from the other, thus leaving the center, very rare, for still rare, even when reheated, second servings.

Reheat rare slices of beef *slowly*—in leftover (or canned) gravy, in small amounts of butter or meat drippings, in barbecue sauce or other sauces. Too much heat too fast and undercooked fibers will contract immediately; the result—dry, tough, and tasteless meat.

To retain all rareness, let slices come to room temperature, place on warm plates, cover with very hot gravy or sauce, and serve at once.

When serving cold beef, bring at least partially to room temperature. Full flavor is masked when meat is overchilled.

BITS AND PIECES

Serve cold sliced beef with hot vegetables, pasta, potatoes, or rice. Use for sandwiches or cold plates.

Add diced or chopped beef to mixed salad, to spaghetti sauce or other sauces.

COLD BEEF STRIPS IN SOUR CREAM

Cut lean rare beef into finger strips. Season with salt, pepper, and a sprinkle of lemon juice. Add enough sour cream to lightly coat meat. Serve as hors d'oeuvre with cocktail picks for spearing.

COLD BEEF ROLLS

Mix 3 parts cream cheese with 1 part horseradish. Spread on thin slices of lean rare beef. Roll up, secure with cocktail picks. Serve as hors d'oeuvre.

COLD BEEF PIQUANTE

Arrange overlapping slices of rare beef on an oval serving platter. Place paper-thin slices of onion over meat. Sprinkle liberally with well-seasoned French or vinaigrette dressing (see page 225). Let stand at room temperature 1 to 2 hours. Just before serving, garnish platter with tomato slices, cold cooked green beans, quartered hard-cooked eggs, and mixed pickles. Serve as main course for a light supper or lunch.

BEEF AU POIVRE WITH MELON

Sprinkle slices of leftover rare beef lightly with salt, heavily with coarsely ground black peppercorns. Press seasoning gently into meat slices. Bring to room temperature. Arrange on serving platter or on individual small plates. Top with thin wedges of ripe cantaloupe, honeydew, or Persian melon. Serve as an appetizer for a formal dinner or as an entree for a light supper or lunch.

RARE BEEF SLICES WITH RED WINE SAUCE

8 *to* 12 *thin slices of rare beef*
2 *to* 3 *shallots, finely chopped*
2 *tablespoons butter*
¾ *cup beef gravy, leftover or canned, or brown sauce* (*see page* 205)

¼ *cup dry red wine*
1 *tablespoon lemon juice*
1 *tablespoon cognac*
Salt
Freshly ground pepper } *to taste*

Bring beef slices to room temperature. Place on heated platter or plates.

Sauté shallots in butter until transparent; add beef gravy and wine. Blend and bring to full boil, then reduce heat and allow to simmer gently 2 to 3 minutes. Add remaining ingredients and season to taste with salt and pepper. Bring again to full boil, pour over meat slices, and serve at once.
[2 *to* 4 *servings.*]

BEEF CHOP SUEY

3 *tablespoons soy sauce*
2 *tablespoons dry sherry*
16 *to* 20 *2-inch strips lean rare roast beef*

1 *teaspoon cornstarch*
2 *teaspoons water*

2 *tablespoons cooking oil*
2 *medium carrots, very thinly sliced, Chinese-fashion, at a 45° angle*
1 *medium turnip, very thinly sliced*

1 *medium sweet red onion, thinly sliced and broken into rings*
8 *to* 10 *medium fresh mushrooms, thinly sliced*
2 *tablespoons water*
1 *teaspoon sugar*
½ *teaspoon salt*
¼ *teaspoon monosodium glutamate*
1 *cup canned bean sprouts, well drained*
½ *cup canned water chestnuts, drained and thinly sliced*

Bring meat to room temperature.

Sprinkle soy sauce and sherry over meat slices; set aside.

Mix cornstarch with water; set aside.

Heat the oil in a large heavy skillet (one with tight-fitting lid). Add the carrots, turnip, onion, and mushrooms all at once. Stir over high heat until all vegetables are well coated with oil—about 2 minutes. Pour the soy sauce and sherry from the meat and add these, with the water, to the vegetables. Add the sugar, salt, and monosodium glutamate. Reduce heat to medium. Cover skillet and cook 2 minutes. Mix in the bean sprouts, water chestnuts, and meat; then gradually add the dissolved cornstarch. Stir and cook only until the meat is hot, sauce thickened (less than a minute).

Serve over just cooked, very hot dry white rice. Have additional soy sauce at the table.

[4 *servings.*]

BEEF STROGANOFF

3 *tablespoons butter*
1 *medium onion, chopped*
1 *small clove garlic, minced*
6 *to 8 fresh mushrooms, thinly sliced*
1 *tablespoon flour*
1 *tablespoon tomato paste*
1½ *cups clear beef stock or bouillon (see page* 202)
2 *to 3 tablespoons beef* jus *(the clear juice from the roasted beef), optional*

2 *tablespoons fresh dill, finely chopped, or generous sprinkling of ground dill*
Salt ⎫
Pepper ⎬ *to taste*
24 *thin strips* (1 x 2 *inches*) *lean, preferably rare, room temperature roast beef*
½ *cup sour cream*
Chopped parsley (optional)

Heat butter in heavy skillet; add onion, garlic, and mushrooms. Cook over moderate heat, stirring frequently, until onion is limp, mushrooms barely cooked through—2 or 3 minutes. Add flour and stir until lightly browned. Stir in tomato paste; when this has been blended in, add stock or bouillon, *jus,* and dill. Season to taste with salt and pepper. Turn heat to very low and cook, stirring frequently, until sauce is thick and smooth. Add meat strips, cook only until they are well heated, then stir in sour cream. Blend well and cook, stirring a final 1 to 2 minutes. Do not allow to boil after adding sour cream. May be served over freshly cooked noodles. Sprinkle with chopped parsley.
[4 *to* 6 *servings.*]

BEEF DIANE

8 *to* 12 *thin slices rare roast beef*
4 *tablespoons butter*
1 *tablespoon lemon juice*
6 *to* 8 *large fresh mushrooms, sliced very thin*
3 *tablespoons Escoffier Sauce Robert* (*commercially bottled*)
1 *tablespoon Worcestershire sauce*
3 *tablespoons cognac or other good brandy*
Salt
Freshly ground black pepper

Allow meat to reach room temperature.

Cook beef slices in butter over medium heat only until thoroughly hot. Remove with spatula or slotted spoon to heated serving plate. Add lemon juice and mushrooms to pan, turn heat to medium high, and cook, stirring frequently, 2 to 3 minutes. Add remaining ingredients, seasoning to taste with salt and freshly ground black pepper. Cook, stirring, only until bubbly hot. Pour over meat slices and serve at once. [4 *to* 6 *servings.*]

NOTE: This method of preparing beef slices lends itself very well to chafing dish—cook at the table—cookery.

ROAST BEEF HASH

1 *medium onion, chopped*
½ *small green pepper, chopped*
4 *tablespoons butter*
2 *cups coarsely chopped lean leftover roast beef*
3 *cups coarsely chopped cold boiled potatoes*
Sufficient beef jus (*the clear juice from the roasted beef*)
*plus enough beef stock or bouillon to make 5 tablespoons**
2 *tablespoons Worcestershire sauce*
Salt
Freshly ground black pepper } *to taste*
1 *tablespoon cooking oil*

Sauté onion and green pepper in 2 tablespoons of the butter until onion is limp but not browned. Combine in mixing bowl with remaining ingredients (except butter and cooking oil). Blend thoroughly but gently using your hands or two forks. Let mixture stand at room temperature 5 to 10 minutes to allow flavoring and liquid to blend with potatoes and meat. Heat remaining butter with oil in a large heavy skillet. Add the hash and pat it down in the pan with a spatula. Cook over moderate heat about 30 minutes. As hash cooks, tip skillet occasionally and remove, with small spoon, any accumulated fat. When hash is brown and crisp on the bottom, place a large plate on top of the skillet and turn the hash out in one piece. If part of the crust sticks to the skillet, remove it with a spatula and patch it into place. Slice in wedges at the table. [4 *servings.*]

* Use all *jus* if desired.

ORIENTAL BEEF

3 *tablespoons butter*
½ *small green pepper, cut in thin strips*
1 *small onion, thinly sliced*
1 *tablespoon curry powder*
16 *to 24 thin strips lean, preferably rare, roast beef 1 x 2 inches*
1 *cup canned pineapple chunks, drained*
2 *cups medium thick cream sauce* (*see page* 207)

1 *firm but ripe avocado, peeled, stoned, and cut into thin wedges*
¼ *cup thinly sliced* (*canned*) *water chestnuts*
1 *or 2 pimiento halves* (*canned*) *cut in narrow strips*
Salt ⎱ *to taste*
Pepper ⎰

Melt the butter in a large heavy skillet. Add green pepper and onion. Sauté over medium heat until onion is limp but not browned. Add curry powder and stir until well blended. Add beef strips. Cook, stirring, until well heated (less than a minute), then add remaining ingredients (except salt and pepper). Fork-stir to avoid breaking up avocado and cook only

until mixture is thoroughly hot. Season to taste with salt and pepper. Serve over freshly cooked hot white rice.
[4 *servings.*]

DEVILED BEEF BONES

Roasted rib beef bones with   *Melted butter*
   some meat   *Fine dry bread crumbs*
Mustard   *Beef gravy (optional)*
Brown sugar

Take the bones from the refrigerator and bring to room temperature.

For each 6 rib bones with some meat, mix together ½ cup prepared mustard, 2 teaspoons brown sugar, and 2 tablespoons melted butter. With a pastry brush or your fingers, paint the entire surface of each bone with this mixture. Then coat each with bread crumbs. Arrange on a rack over a roasting pan and place in a preheated 450° oven for about 20 minutes—until lightly browned. Serve with reheated gravy seasoned with mustard if desired.

Pot Roast of Beef

THOUGH POT ROAST OF BEEF may indeed be used instead of roast beef in the preceding recipes (just as roast beef may be substituted for pot roast in the recipes to follow), this less expensive meat is listed separately because it has special qualities decidedly its own.

To begin with, because a pot roast has been cooked in moist rather than dry heat, it may be subjected to more extensive recooking. Like boiled beef, it may be reheated in its original form without loss of flavor. In addition, its juices and gravies add "flavor plus" when used as the base of any "made from leftovers" dish.

TO STORE: Place in nonmetal bowl or deep dish, pour gravy or cooking juices over surface, and seal bowl or dish with foil. Refrigerate; use within two or three days. Or, follow instructions for storing roast beef; use within time indicated.

BITS AND PIECES

Grind or chop pot roast very fine. Moisten with leftover gravy (fat removed). Season with Worcestershire sauce, Escoffier Sauce Robert, or Escoffier Sauce Diable. Use as spread for hors d'oeuvre.

Mix finely chopped or ground pot roast with finely chopped dill pickles, prepared horseradish, and chopped capers. Moisten with pot roast gravy (fat removed). Mix with equal parts cream cheese. Spread on thin slices of rye bread. Serve for a light lunch or supper, with clear soup or a mixed green salad.

Mash hot freshly boiled potatoes with leftover preheated pot roast gravy instead of butter and cream. Serve with cold or reheated sliced pot roast.

Add 2 or 3 tablespoons of clear pot roast juices or gravy to water when cooking rice. Drain rice, mix with diced leftover pot roast and chopped chives.

BEEF BISCUIT ROLL

2 *cups flour*
½ *teaspoon salt*
2 *teaspoons double-acting baking powder*
¼ *teaspoon rosemary*
5 *tablespoons butter*
6 *to 8 tablespoons ice water*

2 *cups lean diced leftover pot roast*
1 *small onion*

8 *to* 10 *large fresh mushrooms, finely chopped*
2 *to* 3 *tablespoons pot roast gravy*
½ *to* ¾ *cup canned tomato sauce*
Salt ⎱
Pepper ⎰ *to taste*
1 *or* 2 *tablespoons melted butter*
Tomato sauce

Sift flour, salt, baking powder, and rosemary into large mixing bowl. With pastry blender (or your fingers) work in the butter until mixture resembles coarse-ground corn meal. Moisten with sufficient ice water to form a soft dough. Shape into a ball and refrigerate, covered, while preparing filling.

Grind the meat or chop it very fine with the onion. Add mushrooms, beef gravy, and sufficient tomato sauce to form a thick spread. Season to taste with salt and pepper.

Roll out chilled dough about ¼ inch thick on lightly floured board. Trim edges. Spread with meat mixture and roll up (jelly-roll-fashion). Moisten edges with cold water and seal.

Place roll, seam side down, on greased baking sheet. Brush with melted butter. Place in preheated 375° oven and bake, brushing occasionally with additional melted butter, 30 to 35 minutes or until surface is lightly browned. Slice and serve with additional tomato sauce spooned over each portion. [4 *to* 6 *servings.*]

CASSOLETTES DE HACHIS À LA PROVENÇALE
(Hash in individual baking dishes in the style of Provence)

2 *stalks celery, chopped*
½ *small green pepper,*
   chopped
1 *small onion, chopped*
1 *clove garlic, minced*
2 *tablespoons butter*
½ *cup bulk sausage meat*
2 *cups finely diced pot roast of*
   beef
¾ *cup beef gravy, left over*
from roast or canned

1 *tablespoon tomato paste*
Salt ⎫
Freshly ground ⎬ *to taste*
   black pepper ⎭
2 *large fresh tomatoes,*
   chopped
1 *tablespoon olive oil*
6 *eggs*

In large saucepan, sauté the celery, green pepper, onion, and garlic in the butter until limp but not browned. Add the sausage and cook, stirring, over low heat about 5 minutes. Add beef, beef gravy, and tomato paste. Season to taste with salt and pepper. Remove from heat and spoon mixture equally into 6 cassolettes (small ovenproof dishes).

Place the tomatoes in a separate saucepan and cook over medium heat until reduced to a thick pulp. Stir and chop them with the tip of a spatula as they cook. Remove from heat, stir in the olive oil, and season to taste with salt and pepper.

Spread this sauce over the surface of the hash in the cassolettes. With the back of a tablespoon, make a shallow indentation in the center of each dish and break an egg into each indentation. Bake in a 350° preheated oven until eggs have set.

[6 *servings.*]

SHEPHERD'S PIE

2 *cups finely diced pot roast*
¾ *cup gravy from pot roast*
  (or, as substitute, canned
  gravy, or brown sauce, see
  page 205)
1 *small onion, finely minced*
1 *tablespoon tomato paste*

1 *teaspoon Worcestershire*
  sauce
Salt
Freshly ground } *to taste*
  black pepper
Sour cream mashed potatoes—
  see below

Combine beef with gravy, onion, tomato paste, and seasonings. Blend well. Cover the bottom of a well-greased deep baking dish with approximately half of the mashed potatoes. Spoon beef mixture over surface and cover with remaining potatoes. Place in a preheated 350° oven and bake until surface is lightly browned, about 30 minutes.
[4 *to 6 servings.*]

SOUR CREAM MASHED POTATOES

6 *medium potatoes*
3 *tablespoons butter, melted*
  and hot
¼ *cup sour cream, room*
  temperature

Salt
Pepper } *to taste*

Boil potatoes until tender. Drain, peel, and mash with butter and sour cream. Add salt and pepper to taste.

CASSEROLE OF BEEF AND POTATOES

5 *tablespoons butter*
2 *medium boiled potatoes,*
  sliced (leftover or freshly
  cooked)
1 *medium onion, chopped*
1 *small green pepper, chopped*
2 *stalks celery, chopped*

1 *cup canned tomato sauce*
½ *cup beef gravy, preferably*
  leftover
3 *cups diced beef*
Salt
Freshly ground } *to taste*
  black pepper

Melt 3 tablespoons of the butter. Place potatoes in single

layer on a platter or long shallow pan and pour the melted butter over them. Set aside.

In large saucepan sauté onion, green pepper, and celery in remaining butter until limp but not browned. Add the tomato sauce, beef gravy, and beef. Season to taste with salt and pepper. Blend and allow to simmer gently 2 to 3 minutes. Transfer to a casserole or baking dish (one that may be brought to the table) and arrange the buttered potato slices in an attractive overlapping design on top of beef mixture. Bake at 350° 10 to 15 minutes, then place directly under broiler flame until potatoes are lightly browned on top.

COCKTAIL TURNOVERS

2 cups flour
½ teaspoon salt
Generous pinch powdered
  thyme
Generous pinch powdered
  rosemary
½ cup butter
2 tablespoons vegetable
  shortening
2 tablespoons tarragon vinegar
Ice water, about 6 to 8
  tablespoons

1½ cups chopped lean pot
  roast of beef

2 tablespoons minced chives
3 tablespoons finely chopped
  fresh mushrooms
1 tablespoon Marsala wine
2 to 3 tablespoons well-
  seasoned thick gravy from
  pot roast (or, as substitute,
  canned beef gravy well seasoned with salt, pepper, and
  Worcestershire sauce)

1 egg yolk
1 teaspoon milk

Sift flour with salt, thyme, and rosemary. Cut in butter and shortening with a pastry knife (or your fingers) until mixture resembles coarse-ground corn meal. Add vinegar and sufficient ice water to form a smooth ball. Handle dough as lightly and quickly as possible. Refrigerate 30 minutes.

Mix beef with chives, mushrooms, and wine. Add sufficient gravy to bind ingredients.

Roll out dough on a lightly floured board to form a large square. Cut into small squares. Place some of the meat mixture on one side of each, fold over, moisten edges with water, and press together with tines of fork.

Beat egg yolk lightly with milk. Place turnovers, not touching, on baking sheet and brush surface of each with egg yolk mixture. Bake in a preheated 375° oven until lightly browned —about 15 minutes. Serve hot or cold.
[*Makes 12 to 16 small turnovers.*]

BEEF SPREAD FOR CANAPES

¼ *cup Escoffier Sauce Robert (commercially bottled), or, as substitute, H. P. Sauce or any bottled meat sauce of similar consistency*
1 *cup cubed pot roast of beef*
2 *tablespoons clear gravy from pot roast*

1 *small onion, quartered*
¼ *cup sweet mixed pickles*
¼ *clove garlic*
Salt
Freshly ground black pepper } *to taste*

Place all ingredients in container of electric blender. Blend at high speed until smooth. Stop blender when necessary and push ingredients toward blade with rubber spatula.

Or, grind or chop meat very fine with onion, garlic, and pickles. Blend well with Escoffier sauce, gravy, and seasoning.

Refrigerate until well chilled. Store in refrigerator; use within one week.

Spread on French-toast rounds, melba toast, or bland crackers.
[*Makes about 1½ cups.*]

Corned Beef

NOTHING IS QUITE AS SATISFACTORY as corned beef on rye with a crisp pickle and a cold glass of beer—unless it's corned beef reheated in its own cooking juices and served with new boiled potatoes or sauerkraut, or corned beef with mustard on a warm crusty roll. We could go on and on and then on. . . .

Cooked corned beef, like cooked ham, in the refrigerator makes for hearty meals that never fail to please—and can be prepared in almost less time than the telling.

TO STORE: Refrigerate covered in cooking broth; use within two or three days. Or, wrap meat in moistureproof paper; refrigerate up to one week. Or, slice meat, wrap meal-size portions in moistureproof paper, seal, and freeze; store in freezer up to three months.

Reheat whole or sliced corned beef in liquid used in cooking on top the stove—or in medium oven.

Serve cold with hot vegetables, potatoes, or pasta.

Use for sandwiches or cold plates.

Serve with breakfast eggs instead of ham.

THIS AND THAT

Bring unsliced piece (½ lb. or over) of cold corned beef to room temperature. Cover top with brown sugar. Sprinkle with sherry, stick with whole cloves. Bake at 350° until glazed and hot.

Spread dark rye bread with Thousand Island dressing or mayonnaise, cover with slices of Swiss cheese, spread cheese with sauerkraut, cover sauerkraut with slices of corned beef, and top with second slices of bread. Butter outside of bread and grill sandwiches until cheese is melted.

Mix finely diced lean corned beef with equal parts chopped hard-cooked eggs. Season with chopped onion, and bind with mayonnaise thinned with a little good wine vinegar. Add salt and pepper to taste. Serve on lettuce leaves.

Cut cold corned beef into bite-size cubes. Stick each on a cocktail pick with a cube of dill pickle. Serve with a mustard-mayonnaise dip (one part mustard to two parts mayonnaise).

Mix cold thin strips of corned beef with cold cooked lima beans and chopped mild Bermuda onion. Moisten with garlicky French dressing. Spoon into scooped-out tomato shells. Garnish with mayonnaise, and serve on lettuce leaves.

CORNED BEEF CHEESEBURGERS

2 *cups lean cooked corned*
  beef, chopped
3 *tablespoons mustard*
6 *tablespoons mayonnaise*

1 *tablespoon horseradish*
6 *hamburger rolls*
12 *slices Swiss cheese*

Blend chopped corned beef with mustard, mayonnaise, and horseradish. Scoop soft centers from hamburger buns. Toast lightly. Fill with corned beef mixture. Top with slices of Swiss cheese. Place under medium broiler; heat until cheese is melted.

[*Makes 12 open sandwiches.*]

CORNED BEEF HASH

2 cups cooked corned beef,
   finely diced
3 cups boiled potatoes, finely
   diced
Salt ⎫
Freshly ground ⎬ to taste
   black pepper ⎭

1 medium onion, minced
¼ cup beef broth or stock,
   canned or homemade (see
   page 202)
1 tablespoon butter, more if
   needed
1 tablespoon cooking oil

Combine corned beef and potatoes. Season with salt and pepper. Add onion and beef broth or stock.

Heat butter and oil in a heavy skillet. Add the beef-potato mixture and pat down firmly in the pan. Cook without stirring until underside is lightly browned and crispy, adding additional butter if needed. Fold like an omelet, turn out onto serving platter, and serve at once.

[4 to 6 servings.]

CORNED BEEF WITH SAUTÉED CABBAGE

3 tablespoons butter
4 cups cabbage, chopped
   (1 small head)
1 onion, finely chopped
3 tablespoons water
1 tablespoon white wine
   vinegar

2 teaspoons sugar
½ teaspoon salt
¼ teaspoon pepper
6 to 8 slices cooked corned
   beef
Mustard

Melt butter in a large frypan, add chopped cabbage and onion. Moisten with water, vinegar. Add sugar, salt, pepper. Stir to blend, cover, and cook 10 minutes. Arrange slices of corned beef over surface. Spread slices with mustard. Cover and cook until meat is hot, cabbage crisp and tender.

[6 to 8 servings.]

OLD-FASHIONED RED FLANNEL HASH
WITH SALT PORK GRAVY

¼ lb. salt pork, cut into small cubes
6 cold boiled potatoes, diced
1 large onion, chopped
6 cold boiled beets, diced
2 cups diced cooked corned beef
Salt ⎱
Freshly ground ⎬ to taste
  black pepper ⎰

½ cup beef broth from corned beef, or beef stock (see page 202)
1 tablespoon flour
1 cup milk

Cover salt pork with cold water in saucepan. Place over medium heat and bring to boil. Lower heat and simmer 2 minutes, drain and pat dry on paper toweling.

Place in heavy skillet and cook over very low heat until crisp. This will take 20 to 25 minutes. (Do not attempt to "hurry" this process by cooking over high heat or outside of pork will crisp before it is sufficiently cooked.)

Remove pork and set aside. Pour all but about 3 tablespoons of the rendered fat from the skillet. Reserve poured-off fat.

Combine potatoes, onion, beets, and corned beef. Moisten with stock and season to taste with salt and pepper. Blend mixture well and add to skillet. Cover and cook over low heat until underside is crisp and lightly browned. Fold half the hash over the other half and turn it out onto a heated platter. Keep warm while preparing gravy.

Add 2 tablespoons of the reserved fat to the skillet. Stir in the flour and cook, stirring constantly, over low heat until flour is a deep golden brown. Add the milk, slowly stirring it into the flour mixture as it is added. Cook, stirring, until smooth and thick. Add reserved salt pork and cook a final minute. Pour over hash and serve at once.

[6 servings.]

Ham

REBAKE IT IN SAUCE, fry it, combine it with other foods, or serve it cold—the only thing you shouldn't do with leftover ham is to forget it, let it dry out, inadequately wrapped and forgotten, on a back shelf of the refrigerator because your family's "tired of ham this week" and you mistakenly think that this particular meat (unlike any other) will keep indefinitely.

Ham *does* keep well and will taste as delicious as when first served for up to about two weeks after it is cooked—*if* securely wrapped (or placed in an airtight container) and refrigerated. Beyond this period, it will lose flavor, dry out, and in time become moldy. It may, of course, be stored in the freezer, where it will stay moist, juicy, and fresh three months or longer—but again, only if properly wrapped to seal out all air and moisture.

TO STORE: Wrap leftover ham with bone in foil or plastic wrap, or place in airtight container; refrigerate up to two weeks. Or, slice from bone, remove all fat, wrap in meal-size portions, and store in freezer up to three months.

HAM SLICES PIQUANTE

8 *to* 12 *thick slices boiled or*   *Brown sugar*
   baked ham   *Port or Madeira wine*
Dijon mustard

Bring ham slices to room temperature. For each slice mix together 1 tablespoon each mustard and sugar. Moisten with enough wine to make a smooth paste. Spread on ham slices. Arrange slices in shallow baking dish. Place about 3 or 4 inches under broiler heat. Broil until surface is glazed.
[4 *servings.*]

BAKED HAM IN CREAM

8 *to* 12 *thin slices of boiled or baked ham (fat removed)*   4 *to* 6 *teaspoons dry mustard*
1 *cup heavy cream*

Spread each slice of ham with about ½ teaspoon dry mustard, pressing it into the ham. Place in overlapping slices in a shallow baking dish. Cover with cream. Bake in a 350° preheated oven for 15 to 20 minutes.
[4 *to* 6 *servings.*]

LOUISIANA HAM AND OYSTER JAMBALAYA

2 *tablespoons peanut or corn oil*
1 *small clove garlic, minced*
1 *medium onion, chopped*
1 *small green pepper, chopped, free of all seeds and fiber*
1 *cup Italian short-grain rice (or, as substitute, 1 cup long-grain rice)*
3½ *cups chicken stock or bouillon, canned or home-made, free of fat*
½ *teaspoon salt*

1½ *cups canned tomatoes, preferably Italian-style with basil, chopped but not drained*
1 *cup diced boiled or baked ham*
1 *bay leaf*
⅛ *teaspoon saffron (optional)*
Salt
Freshly ground black pepper } *to taste*
1 *dozen oysters and their liquid*

Heat the oil in a deep heavy saucepan (one with a tight-fitting lid). Add the garlic, onion, and green pepper. Stir over medium heat until vegetables are limp but not browned. Add rice and continue stirring until all grains are coated with oil.

In separate saucepan bring stock or bouillon to a full boil. Add the salt and pour over rice and vegetables. Add remaining ingredients except oysters. Cover pan and allow to simmer over very low heat for 25 to 30 minutes or until rice is tender and has absorbed all liquid.

If onion and green pepper were particularly watery, the rice may become too soft before absorbing all liquid. If so, remove lid and place the pot in a 200° oven for 10 or 15 minutes. This should dry out the rice sufficiently.

Heat the oysters in their own liquid in a separate pan for 1 to 2 minutes or until edges begin to curl. Add them to the jambalaya, fork-stir to blend. Correct seasoning with additional salt and pepper if needed, and serve.

[4 *to* 6 *servings.*]

HAM AND SPAGHETTI WITH FRESH TOMATOES

2 *medium tomatoes, cut into thin wedges*
½ *medium green pepper, seeded and cut into strips*
¼ *cup olive oil*
6 *to* 8 *scallions, cut into* 1-*inch pieces*

20 *to* 24 *thin strips of cooked ham*
½ *teaspoon dried or fresh basil*
Salt
Pepper } *to taste*
1 1-*lb. package spaghetti*
⅓ *cup grated Parmesan cheese*

Cook the tomato slices and green pepper in the olive oil over low heat only until hot. Add the scallions and ham. Season with basil, salt, and pepper. Cook, stirring very gently (so tomato wedges do not break), until ham is well heated.

Cook spaghetti according to package directions. Drain, combine with ham mixture. Sprinkle with Parmesan cheese, and serve.

[4 *servings.*]

HAM AND CHEESE LOAF

1 *long loaf French bread*
¾ *cup diced boiled or baked ham*
¾ *cup grated Swiss cheese*
¼ *cup butter, melted*
1 *clove garlic, finely minced*

1 *small onion, finely chopped*
¼ *cup chopped pimiento-stuffed olives*
¼ *teaspoon freshly ground black pepper*

Slice off top third of French bread. Scoop out soft center and save a sufficient amount to make about ½ cup fine crumbs. Combine these with remaining ingredients. Mix well and stuff the hollowed-out center with the mixture. Cover with top portion of loaf, brush with melted butter. Wrap in foil.

Bake in a preheated 350° oven for 30 minutes or until well heated. Cut into slices and serve.

[4 *to* 6 *servings.*]

BRAISED HAM SLICES IN PORT WINE WITH CREAM SAUCE

2 *tablespoons butter*
1 *medium onion, chopped*
1 *medium carrot, scrapped and chopped*
2 *stalks celery, chopped*
4 *to* 6 *thick slices of boiled or baked ham*

1 *cup port wine*
1 *cup heavy cream*
Paprika
Cayenne pepper } *to taste*
Salt

Heat the butter in a large ovenproof skillet. Add the vegetables and cook, stirring, over low heat for 2 to 3 minutes. Arrange ham slices over vegetables, pour ¼ cup of the port over them, and transfer skillet to a preheated 350° oven. Bake for 30 minutes, basting frequently with the remaining port.

Remove ham slices to a heated platter. Cook the sauce over moderate heat until reduced by half. Lower heat, stir in cream, and cook, stirring, for about 5 minutes. Do not allow to boil. Season to taste with paprika, pepper, and salt. Pour over ham slices.

[4 *servings.*]

COLD HAM MOUSSE WITH SPICY FRUIT SALAD

1 *package* (1 *tablespoon*) *unflavored gelatin*
⅓ *cup cold water*
2 *cups finely ground cooked
ham*
½ *cup finely minced celery*
¼ *cup finely minced green
pepper*

¼ *cup finely minced green
onion*
1 *cup heavy cream*
2 *tablespoons Madeira wine*
Spicy fruit salad—see below

Sprinkle gelatin over cold water to soften. Place over very low heat and stir constantly until dissolved. Remove from heat, add ham, celery, pepper, and onion; blend well. Beat cream until stiff. Add Madeira and fold into ham mixture. Spoon into a well-greased ring mold and refrigerate until chilled and firm. Unmold onto round platter and fill center with spicy fruit salad.
[6 *to* 8 *servings.*]

SPICY FRUIT SALAD

4 *pickled peaches, sliced*
2 *ripe bananas, peeled and
sliced*
1 *medium avocado, peeled
and sliced*
2 *tablespoons lemon juice*

2 *tablespoons minced chives*
2 *tablespoons minced parsley*
¼ *cup mayonnaise*
1 *tablespoon juice from
peaches*

Combine fruit, sprinkle with lemon juice, chives, and parsley. Mix mayonnaise with peach juice. Add to fruit and place salad mixture in center of ham mousse.

HOT HAM MOUSSE

1 *cup milk*
1 *cup soft bread crumbs*
2 *cups very finely ground ham*
(put through food chopper 3 times)

4 *eggs, separated*
Salt ⎫
Pepper ⎬ *to taste*

Combine milk and bread crumbs in saucepan, bring almost to boil. Remove from heat and cool slightly. Add ham in mixing bowl, stir in egg yolks, and season lightly with salt and pepper. Blend well. Beat egg whites until stiff, fold into ham mixture, pour into a well-greased 2-quart mold. Place mold in larger pan of warm water. Bake in preheated 375° oven until firm (about 30 minutes). Serve with mushroom sauce (see page 206).
[6 *servings.*]

BAKED HAM AND EGGS

1 *small onion, chopped*
½ *small green pepper, seeded and chopped*
2 *tablespoons butter*
3¾ *cups minced boiled or baked ham*

8 *eggs*
4 *teaspoons cream*
Butter slivers
Salt ⎫
Pepper ⎬ *to taste*

Sauté onion and green pepper in butter until limp but not browned. Add ham and blend well.

Spoon mixture into 4 buttered ramekins or individual soufflé dishes. Break 2 eggs into each and spoon 1 teaspoon cream over surface. Dot with slivers of butter. Sprinkle with salt and pepper and bake in a preheated 350° oven until eggs have set (about 12 minutes).
[4 *servings.*]

HAM AND BOILED BEANS

4 *cups navy beans*	*Sprig of parsley*
Water	1 *bay leaf*
Ham bone from boiled or	1 *teaspoon sugar*
baked ham with some meat	3 *tablespoons tomato paste*
and a little fat	*Salt* ⎫
1 *large onion, stuck with*	*Pepper* ⎬ *to taste*
1 *clove*	⎭

Wash beans. Cover with cold water and soak overnight.

Place ham bone in large heavy pot. Add beans and water in which they soaked. Add sufficient fresh water if needed to cover ham bone and beans. Add onion, parsley, bay leaf, and sugar.

Heat slowly and cook over low heat until beans are tender (1½ to 2 hours).

Remove ham bone. Cut off any remaining meat and add to pot. Remove bay leaf and parsley. Stir in tomato paste, season to taste with salt and pepper. Cook a final 10 to 15 minutes. [6 *servings.*]

Lamb

As INGENIOUS COOKS of both Europe and the Middle East have long known, lamb lends itself particularly well to reheating. Even when subjected to lengthy recooking, it retains its distinctive flavor and remains tender. Besides this, it takes only a little leftover lamb to make a truly epicurean dish.

T O S T O R E : Roast lamb—follow instructions for roast beef. Braised lamb—follow instructions for pot roast of beef.

BITS AND PIECES

Add thin strips of cold lamb to green salad or to cooked vegetable salad. Add to clear soup.

Dice lamb, bind with rich cream sauce. Serve hot over old-fashioned baking powder biscuits as you would creamed chicken.

Spread bread first with currant jelly, then with ground or finely diced lamb. Cover with second slice of bread spread with hot mustard. Toast sandwich on both sides. Spoon hot lamb gravy over surface. Serve as luncheon entree.

Mix diced cold lamb with mild Bermuda onions. Moisten with French dressing. Refrigerate covered for 2 to 3 hours. Drain. Spoon onto crisp lettuce leaves, top with a bit of mayonnaise. Serve as a main-course salad.

LAMB CROQUETTES WITH BAR-LE-DUC SAUCE

3 *tablespoons butter*
3 *tablespoons flour*
¾ *cup beef broth or stock,*
   canned or homemade
Salt ⎱ *to taste*
Pepper ⎰
1 *teaspoon Escoffier Sauce*
   Diable (commercially
   bottled)
1 *teaspoon Bar-le-Duc jelly*
   (imported currant jelly)
½ *cup finely minced mush-*
   rooms

2 *tablespoons finely minced*
   parsley
3 *cups ground (or very finely*
   minced) cooked lamb
2 *egg yolks, lightly beaten*

Flour, about ⅓ *cup*
1 *egg, beaten with 2 table-*
   spoons milk
Fine dry bread crumbs, about
   1 *cup*

Melt butter in large saucepan. Stir in flour; when mixture is bubbly, gradually add stock and stir until smooth. Season to taste with salt and pepper. Add Sauce Diable and Bar-le-Duc jelly. Stir until blended and add mushrooms, parsley, and lamb. Remove pan from heat, cool slightly, then stir in egg yolks. Reduce heat and cook, stirring, until mixture is quite thick. Pour into a long shallow pan. Refrigerate until well chilled.

Shape the chilled mixture into small cylinders or cones. Roll them first in flour, then in egg mixture, and finally in bread crumbs. Refrigerate again until well chilled and firm.

Fry croquettes a few at a time in hot deep fat until lightly browned. Drain on paper toweling. Serve with Bar-le-Duc sauce.

[6 *servings.*]

BAR-LE-DUC SAUCE

⅓ cup brown sugar
¾ cup Bar-le-Duc jelly
    (imported currant jelly)

1 tablespoon dry mustard
4 egg yolks
½ cup white wine vinegar

Combine sugar, jelly, mustard, and egg yolks in top of double boiler. Cook over simmering water, stirring constantly, until thick and smooth. Add vinegar 1 tablespoon at a time, stirring after each addition. Blend well and serve warm with lamb croquettes.

MOUSSAKA

4 medium eggplants
4 tablespoons olive oil
    (approximately)
2 to 2½ cups ground or finely
    minced cooked lamb
4 tablespoons butter
½ cup finely diced mushrooms
¼ cup finely diced shallots
1 small clove garlic, minced
½ cup leftover lamb gravy (fat
    removed), or, as substitute,

if desired, canned beef gravy
    or brown sauce (see page
    206)
3 tablespoons tomato purée
2 to 3 dashes of Tabasco sauce
2 tablespoons minced parsley
Salt
Freshly ground   } to taste
    black pepper
2 eggs, lightly beaten
Rich tomato sauce

Cut the eggplants in half lengthwise. Heat the oil in a heavy skillet. Add the eggplants, skin side up, and cook over moderate heat 5 to 7 minutes. Remove from skillet, scoop out the meat, and chop it very fine. Reserve the skins.

Combine the chopped eggplant with the lamb. Set aside. Pour the oil from the skillet and wipe pan clean with paper toweling. Add the butter. When this has melted, add the mushrooms, shallots, and garlic. Cook, stirring, over moderate heat until mushrooms and shallots are limp. Remove skillet from heat and add the lamb-eggplant mixture, the lamb gravy, tomato purée, Tabasco sauce, and parsley. Season to taste with salt and pepper, stir in the eggs, and blend well.

Cut the eggplant skins lengthwise into wide even slices. Grease a charlotte or timbale mold generously with mild oil and line it completely with some of the eggplant skins, purple side down. Fill with the lamb-eggplant mixture and cover with rest of eggplant skins, purple side up, tucking them into the sides of the mold so that the filling is completely enclosed.

Place the mold in a large pan of warm water, and bake in a preheated 375° oven until firm—45 minutes to 1 hour.

Remove from oven and let stand a few moments. Unmold onto a hot serving plate. Serve with tomato sauce.

[6 *to* 8 *servings.*]

PAPOUTSAKIA
(Greek Lamb-stuffed Eggplant)

4 *medium eggplants*
2 *teaspoons salt*
4 *tablespoons butter*
1 *tablespoon olive oil*
1 *medium onion, chopped*
1 *small clove garlic, minced*
¾ *cup finely diced cooked lamb*
¾ *cup cooked white rice*
½ *cup canned tomato sauce*
2 *tablespoons tomato purée*

1 *teaspoon salt*
¼ *teaspoon freshly ground black pepper*
3 *tablespoons grated sharp cheese*
3 *tablespoons fine dry bread crumbs*
3 *tablespoons melted butter*
1 *cup boiling water*

Cut eggplants in half lengthwise. With a sharp knife make fairly deep crisscross incisions in the flesh, being careful not to cut through the skins. Sprinkle each half with ½ teaspoon of salt and let stand for 30 minutes. Drain off the juices, dry the cut surfaces, and scoop out the pulp. Set aside.

Heat 2 tablespoons of the butter and the olive oil in a deep heavy skillet. Add the eggplant shells, cover, and cook over moderate heat until they start to soften. Transfer them to a long shallow baking dish.

Add the remaining butter, the onion, and the garlic to the skillet and cook, stirring, until onion is limp. Add the egg-

plant pulp and cook a few minutes longer. Remove from heat and stir in the lamb, rice, tomato sauce, and tomato purée. Season with salt and pepper. Blend well and spoon mixture into the eggplant shells. Sprinkle surfaces with grated cheese and bread crumbs, drizzle with melted butter. Pour a cup of boiling water into bottom of pan and cover with aluminum foil. Place in a preheated 350° oven and bake covered, for 45 minutes. Remove foil and bake until top of lamb mixture is lightly browned.
[6 *servings.*]

DOLMADAKIA ME AVGOLEMONO
(Greek Lamb-stuffed Grape Leaves with Lemon-Egg Sauce)

1 1-*lb. jar grape leaves*
2 *tablespoons olive oil*
1 *tablespoon butter*
1 *large onion, chopped*
1 *small clove garlic, minced*
1 *cup finely diced or ground cooked lamb*
¾ *cup uncooked long-grain rice*
1 *teaspoon crumbled mint leaves*
2 *tablespoons coarsely chopped pine nuts*

⅛ *teaspoon allspice*
1 *teaspoon salt*
½ *teaspoon pepper*
2 *to* 2½ *cups chicken stock*

2 *tablespoons melted butter*
2 *egg yolks*
⅓ *cup lemon juice*
Salt to taste

Drain brine from grape leaves and wash them well in clear water to remove all traces of brine. Separate leaves gently and spread them out on paper toweling to dry.

Heat the oil and butter in a large saucepan, add the onion and garlic, and sauté over moderate heat until vegetables are limp. Remove from heat and stir in lamb, rice, mint, pine nuts, and seasoning.

Place grape leaves, glossy side down, on a flat surface and spoon a little filling on each. Roll each leaf tightly, folding edges in and rolling toward point of leaf.

Cover bottom of long shallow pan with crumbled grape leaves and place filled leaves in layers on top.

Heat chicken stock to boiling, pour over prepared grape leaves. Pour melted butter over surfaces. Place a heavy platter or plate directly on top of rolls to keep them from opening as the rice expands. Cover pan with aluminum foil and seal by pressing foil to sides of pan. Place in a preheated 350° oven and bake for 1 hour.

Transfer rolls to heated platter. Keep warm. Keep stock in baking pan hot. Beat the egg yolks until very light, then beat in the lemon juice and beat a full minute. Add 3 tablespoons of the hot stock from the baking pan, blend well, and season to taste with salt. Pour over the stuffed grape leaves, and serve at once.

[6 *servings.*]

ARMENIAN LAMB PILAF

1 *tablespoon butter*
1 *tablespoon olive oil*
1 *cup uncooked imported Italian short-grain rice*
2 *tablespoons minced green onion*
4 *cups beef broth or stock, canned or homemade, free of all fat*
Salt ⎤
Freshly ground ⎬ *to taste*
  black pepper ⎦

2 *tablespoons butter*
1 *large sweet red onion, chopped*
1 *medium green pepper, cut into strips, free of all seed and fiber*

1 *clove garlic, minced*
2 *to 2½ cups diced cooked lamb*
2 *to 3 tablespoons unthickened juice from cooked lamb (substitute beef broth or stock if necessary)*
½ *cup chopped pine nuts*
½ *cup currants, washed and drained*
½ *teaspoon monosodium glutamate*
⅛ *teaspoon cinnamon*
¼ *teaspoon ground allspice*
Salt ⎤
Freshly ground ⎬ *to taste*
  black pepper ⎦
1 *tablespoon chopped fresh mint leaves, or 1 teaspoon dried mint leaves*

Heat the butter and oil in a deep heavy saucepan (one with a tight-fitting cover). Add rice and stir with wooden spoon over fairly low heat until grains are thoroughly coated with butter and oil. Do not allow rice to brown. Add green onion and cook, stirring, until onion is limp—do not allow to brown. In separate pan bring stock to boil, season to taste with salt and pepper, and pour over rice. Cook over medium heat until rice is tender and all liquid has been absorbed— 25 to 35 minutes.

While rice cooks, heat the 2 tablespoons butter in a heavy skillet. Add onion, green pepper, and garlic. Cook, stirring frequently, over medium heat until vegetables are limp but not browned. Add remaining ingredients except mint. Cover skillet and cook over very low heat for 10 to 15 minutes. Stir in mint. Keep hot until rice is cooked, or reheat. Combine with rice, toss lightly, and serve.

[4 *to* 6 *servings.*]

LAMB PATTIES WITH RED CURRANT SAUCE

2 *cups diced cooked lamb*
3 *medium or* 2 *large Idaho potatoes (approximately* 1 *lb.)*
1 *medium onion, chopped*
2 *tablespoons butter*
1 *egg, lightly beaten*
½ *teaspoon salt*

1 *tablespoon Escoffier Sauce Diable (commercially bottled), or, as substitute,* 1 *tablespoon Worcestershire sauce*
Flour
Butter
Red currant sauce (see page 40)

Grind or mince lamb very fine. Boil potatoes until tender. Peel and mash. Sauté onion in butter until limp but not browned. Combine in mixing bowl with lamb and potatoes, egg, salt, and Sauce Diable. Blend well. Cool and shape into 12 small balls. Roll each ball lightly in flour and flatten into a patty. Heat a small amount of butter in a heavy skillet. Fry patties a few at a time until browned on both sides. Keep

warm in 200° oven until all patties are cooked. Serve with
red currant sauce.
[4 *to* 6 *servings.*]

NOTE: Patties may be prepared ahead. Refrigerate covered until ready
to cook.

RED CURRANT SAUCE

1 *cup red currant jelly*   ⅓ *teaspoon grated lemon rind*
1 *to* 2 *tablespoons prepared*   ¼ *cup chopped fresh mint*
  horseradish   *leaves*

Soften jelly over hot water. Add horseradish, lemon rind,
and mint leaves. Serve warm.
[*Makes about* 1⅛ *cup sauce.*]

EASY LAMB CURRY

1⅓ *cups milk*   *Salt*
¾ *cup coconut (canned)*   *Freshly ground* } *to taste*
3 *tablespoons butter*   *black pepper*
1 *tablespoon curry powder*   2 *cups diced cooked lamb*
2 *tablespoons flour*   ½ *cup chutney (Major Gray*
1½ *cups clear beef stock,*   *variety) with large pieces cut*
  canned or homemade (see   *into bite size*
  page 202)   *Cooked rice*

Place milk and coconut in electric blender. Blend until
smooth. Set aside.

Melt butter in large saucepan over low heat. Stir in curry
powder and flour. When these are thoroughly blended, slowly
add stock, stirring it into the flour mixture as it is added. Add
prepared coconut milk, season with salt and pepper. Cook,
stirring, until sauce is thick and smooth. Add lamb and chutney. Cook until lamb is thoroughly heated. Serve over cooked
rice.
[4 *servings.*]

Pork

FRESH PORK in these United States is better than ever—leaner, juicier, and more tasty. Braised pork tenderloin is an especially good choice for the "cook ahead" cook, but so is a roast half of fresh ham. In fact, all pork can be reheated with equal success, and each cut makes for delicious cold eating.

TO STORE: Wrap and refrigerate or freeze cooked leftover pork as you would ham (see page 26).

BITS AND PIECES

Serve cold thinly sliced pork with mustard pickles, pickled peaches or pears, fresh slices of pineapple, or with hot creamed vegetables, hot baked potatoes, cold potato salad, cole slaw, or hot sauerkraut.

Cut cooked pork into thick small slices. Heat in barbecue sauce. Serve from chafing dish, with cocktail picks for spearing.

Cut cooked pork into bite-size cubes. Serve as an appetizer on small cocktail plates, 4 or 5 cubes per plate. Add a bit of prepared Chinese mustard and the same amount of bottled Chinese plum sauce* to each plate for dunking.

Spear halved preserved kumquats (drained) and cubes of roasted pork on cocktail picks. Serve with a dip of prepared Chinese mustard.

Cut cold roasted pork into bite-size cubes. Serve with:

* Available in Chinese markets or gourmet food shops.

CHINESE SOUR CREAM DIP

1 *cup sour cream*   2 *tablespoons chili sauce*
¼ *cup Hoisin Sauce* (*available*
  in Chinese groceries)

Combine ingredients. Blend well. Serve chilled.

JELLIED PORK LOAF WITH APPLESAUCE

2 *envelopes gelatin*   1 *hard-cooked egg, thinly*
¼ *cup cold water*   *sliced*
1½ *cups chicken stock*   2½ *cups chopped cold cooked*
  (*see page* 203)   *pork*
½ *cup Madeira wine*   ½ *cup applesauce*
6 *pimiento-stuffed green olives,* *Mayonnaise*
  sliced   *Pimiento strips*

Sprinkle gelatin over cold water and let stand for 5 minutes.
Heat stock to boiling. Remove from heat, add softened gelatin, and stir until dissolved. Add Madeira and cool to luke-
warm. Pour enough of the cooled mixture into a lightly greased
1½-quart mold to cover bottom. Arrange sliced olives and
hard-cooked egg in attractive design over surface. Refrigerate
until firm.

Combine pork and applesauce, blend, and add to mold al-
ternately with remaining gelatin mixture. Refrigerate until firm.

Dip mold briefly in hot water and unmold onto serving
platter. Garnish with mayonnaise and strips of pimiento.
[6 *servings.*]

EMPANADAS (WITH PORK)
(South American Meat Turnovers)

Flaky pastry for 24 *small turnovers* (*see page* 220)

2 *tablespoons olive oil*
1 *small onion, chopped*
1 *teaspoon flour*
1 8-*oz. can tomato sauce*
½ *teaspoon chili powder*
Dash of cumin powder
¼ *cup seedless raisins, plumped in* ¼ *cup water and drained*

2 *tablespoons finely chopped candied citron*
¼ *cup chopped blanched and toasted almonds*
1½ *cups finely diced cooked pork*
Oil for frying, or cold milk (*if empanadas are to be baked*)

Prepare dough for pastry and roll into a ball. Refrigerate in covered bowl.

Heat oil in a heavy skillet, add onion, and sauté until limp. Stir in flour. When this is blended, add tomato sauce, chili powder, and cumin. Blend these in and add remaining ingredients except frying oil. Cook, stirring, over low heat until sauce is quite thick. Remove from heat and cool.

Roll out chilled prepared dough on lightly floured board. Cut with pastry cutter or knife into small circles (about 3 inches in diameter). Place a small amount of the cooled filling on each circle. Fold over, moisten edges with a little cold water, and press together with the tines of a fork. Refrigerate until well chilled.

Fill a deep heavy pot with oil to within about 3 inches of rim. Heat to 365° on deep-fat thermometer (or until small cube of soft white bread will brown in 30 seconds). Add the empanadas a few at a time and fry until lightly browned. Drain on paper toweling.

If preferred, empanadas may be baked. Place on cookie sheet, brush with a little cold milk, and prick the tops with a

fork. Place in a preheated 375° oven until lightly browned—
about 15 minutes.

Empanadas may be prepared ahead, refrigerated or frozen,
and then fried or baked as needed.

Serve warm as appetizer or hors d'oeuvre.
[*Makes about* 24 *small turnovers.*]

SAUERKRAUT WITH APPLE CIDER, PINEAPPLE, AND PORK

2 *lbs. sauerkraut*	1 *small can pineapple chunks,*
3 *cups apple cider*	*drained*
1 *cup diced roasted pork*	

Drain and wash sauerkraut under cold running water. Place
in saucepan with apple cider. Cook over low heat for ½ hour.
Add pork, stirring it into the kraut. Cover. Cook 15 minutes.
Add pineapple and cook a final 10 minutes.
[6 *to* 8 *servings.*]

QUICK PORK AND BEANS

1 *can* (1 *lb.* 12 *oz.*) *baked beans*	1 *teaspoon dry mustard*
2 *tablespoons tarragon vinegar*	1 *cup diced roasted pork*
2 *tablespoons brown sugar*	*Salt* ⎫ *to taste*
	Pepper ⎭

Combine all ingredients. Place in deep casserole. Cover and
bake in 350° oven until thoroughly heated.
[4 *servings.*]

CHINESE PORK WITH VEGETABLES

1 *tablespoon butter*
2 *tablespoons peanut or corn oil*
2 *cups cold diced roast pork*
2 *medium carrots, scraped and very thinly sliced, Chinese-fashion, at a 45° angle*
1 *medium turnip, peeled and thinly sliced, each slice cut in half*
1 *medium sweet red onion, diced*
1 *small can mixed Chinese vegetables, well drained*
1 *small can water chestnuts, well drained and thinly sliced*
1 *tablespoon water*
3 *tablespoons soy sauce*
Salt to taste
Cooked rice

Heat the butter with the oil in a large heavy skillet. Add the pork and cook, stirring, over high heat about 1 minute or until any bits of fat on the pork are crisp. Add remaining ingredients, fork-stir to blend. Cover skillet and cook over medium heat only until carrots and turnip are crisp-tender. This will take less than 10 minutes if vegetables have been cut sufficiently thin.

Uncover skillet and stir mixture several times as it cooks. Add a small quantity of additional water or soy sauce if needed, but just a little. When dish is ready to serve, meat and vegetables should be moist but there should be only a small amount of liquid. Serve over very hot freshly cooked white rice.

[4 *servings.*]

PORK WITH SWEET-AND-SOUR SAUCE

2 *cups diced lean pork (bite-size pieces)*
1 *tablespoon vegetable oil*
1 *clove garlic, split*
1 *small green pepper, seeded and cut into 1-inch strips*
1 *cup clear chicken stock or broth*
2 *tablespoons red wine vinegar*

1 *tablespoon brown sugar*
1 *tablespoon soy sauce*
1 *small can pineapple chunks with juice*
½ *cup sweet mixed pickles*
2 *teaspoons cornstarch dissolved in 1 tablespoon water*
1 *small firm but ripe tomato cut into 8 wedges*
White rice

Bring pork to room temperature. Heat the oil with the garlic. Add the green pepper, cook over moderate heat for 1 minute. Remove garlic and add stock, vinegar, sugar, soy sauce and juice from pineapple. Bring to boil, add pineapple chunks, pickles, and pork. Cook for 2 to 3 minutes, stir in cornstarch, blend, and add tomato wedges. Cook a final minute. Serve over freshly cooked dry and fluffy white rice.
[2 *servings.*]

EGGS FOO YOUNG WITH PORK

2 *tablespoons chopped scallions*
¼ *cup thinly sliced celery*
3 *tablespoons corn oil*
¼ *cup thinly sliced (canned) water chestnuts, well drained*
½ *cup finely shredded cooked lean pork*

1 *tablespoon soy sauce*
1 *teaspoon salt*
1 *teaspoon sugar*
6 *eggs*
Sherry soy sauce (see page 47)

In saucepan sauté the scallions and celery in 1 tablespoon of the corn oil for 1 minute. Add the water chestnuts, pork, soy sauce, salt, and sugar. Blend well, remove from heat, and set aside until cool.

Beat the eggs until frothy and combine with the cooled

pork mixture. Heat about 1 teaspoon of the remaining oil in a 5- to 6-inch omelet pan. Pour in about one sixth of the egg mixture. Cook over medium flame until underside is lightly browned. Turn and brown second side. Transfer to a heated platter and repeat until all egg mixture has been used.

Serve omelet cakes with a little sherry soy sauce spooned over each.

[*Makes 6 small omelet cakes.*]

SHERRY SOY SAUCE

¾ *cup clear chicken broth or stock*
1 *clove garlic, split*
2 *tablespoons semisweet sherry*
1 *tablespoon soy sauce*
2 *teaspoons cornstarch dissolved in 1 tablespoon water*

Combine stock and garlic in saucepan. Bring to boil. Remove garlic and add sherry and soy sauce. Simmer gently 3 to 4 minutes. Add cornstarch and stir until sauce thickens.

Tongue

ALMOST EVERYONE likes cold boiled tongue—in sandwiches, salads, and "platters," with mustard and plain. In fact, cold tongue is so satisfactory that often it's forgotten that, like all boiled and cured meats, tongue may also be reheated with equal success.

TO STORE: Cool boiled tongue at room temperature in cooking juices. Then remove from liquid and pat dry. Wrap in foil or store in airtight container; refrigerate up to one week. Or, slice and wrap in meal-size portions. Wrap in foil or place in airtight container and freeze; store in freezer up to three months.

BITS AND PIECES

Add julienne strips of cold boiled tongue to chef's salads, to tomato sauce for pasta, to clear soups, or to any canned meat- or vegetable-based soup.

Spread thin slices of tongue with anchovy butter (1 part anchovy paste creamed with 2 parts soft butter). Roll up, secure with cocktail picks, and serve as an appetizer.

Cut cold tongue into bite-size cubes. Serve with cocktail spears for dunking into:

HOT CHEESE DIP

1 *cup shredded sharp cheddar cheese*	1 *split clove of garlic* *Salt* ⎫ *Pepper* ⎭ *to taste*
¾ *cup beer or ale, more as needed*	

Combine all ingredients in chafing dish over hot water. Stir until blended and smooth. Keep warm over hot water. Stir occasionally. Add more beer if mixture becomes too thick.

TONGUE IN MADEIRA SAUCE

2 *tablespoons butter*
1 *tablespoon flour*
1 *cup beef stock*
  (*see page* 202)
½ *cup Madeira wine*

8 *to* 12 *thick slices of boiled tongue*
Salt ⎫
Pepper ⎭ *to taste*

Melt butter in a heavy skillet. Stir in flour. Cook, stirring, over very low heat until mixture turns a deep golden brown. Add stock slowly, stirring it into the (flour-butter) roux as it is added. When mixture is blended, add Madeira, cook, stirring, until sauce begins to thicken. Add tongue slices and continue to cook only until slices are thoroughly heated. Season with salt and pepper.
[4 *servings.*]

TONGUE IN CRANBERRY SAUCE

8 *to* 12 *thick slices of boiled tongue*
½ *cup sugar*
½ *cup water*
½ *cup cranberries*
2 *tablespoons butter*
2 *tablespoons minced onion*

2 *tablespoons flour*
1 *cup cooking liquid from tongue, or, as substitute, beef stock* (*see page* 202)
Salt ⎫
Pepper ⎭ *to taste*

Take tongue from refrigerator, bring to room temperature.

Combine sugar and water in saucepan. Cook, stirring, until sugar dissolves. Add cranberries and bring to boil; lower heat and simmer gently until cranberries begin to burst. Remove from heat. Set aside.

Melt butter in a second saucepan, add onion, and sauté until limp. Stir in flour. When this is blended in, add stock, stirring it into the flour mixture as it is added. Cook, stirring, until sauce is thick and smooth. Season with salt and pepper and remove from heat.

Drain cranberries and add to sauce.

Arrange tongue slices in a shallow baking dish, pour cranberry sauce over surface. Place in preheated 375° oven for 12 to 15 minutes or until tongue is thoroughly heated. [4 *servings*.]

TONGUE WITH BLACKBERRY GLAZE

8 *to* 12 *thick slices of tongue*
½ *cup seedless raisins*
2 *tablespoons cognac or other good brandy*
½ *cup blackberry jam*
1 *tablespoon lemon juice*

Remove tongue from refrigerator, bring to room temperature.

Pour a cup of boiling water over raisins. Let stand 30 minutes. Drain and add cognac or other brandy.

Melt blackberry jam in top half of double boiler over simmering water. Add raisins-cognac mixture and lemon juice.

Arrange tongue slices in shallow baking dish. Pour melted jam sauce over surface. Place in preheated 375° oven until tongue is heated and glazed with jam sauce—about 15 minutes. [4 *servings*.]

SLICED TONGUE WITH SWEET-AND-SOUR SAUCE

1 *tablespoon butter or oil*
6 *scallions, diced*
1 *tablespoon flour*
1 *cup beef consommé*
2 *tablespoons vinegar*
¼ *cup honey*
½ *teaspoon salt*
4 *to* 6 *pieces of candied ginger, cut into thin strips*
¼ *cup seedless raisins*
¼ *cup slivered blanched almonds*
12 *thick-cut slices of tongue*

Heat butter or oil in a heavy saucepan. Add the scallions. Cook, stirring, for ½ minute. Stir in the flour, then slowly

add the beef consommé. Cook, stirring, until mixture begins
to thicken. Add vinegar, honey, salt, ginger, and raisins. Cook
over low heat for 5 minutes. Add almonds and tongue slices.
Cook 2 minutes longer.
[6 *servings.*]

Veal

WE AMERICANS tend to forget veal—which is rather a shame. Properly cooked, it is a tender, moist, and flavorful meat that can be served with pride the second time as well as the first.

TO STORE: For roast veal follow the instructions for roast beef (page 8). For braised veal follow the instructions for pot roast of beef (page 16).

BITS AND PIECES

Cold veal may be used in place of cold lamb or pork (see pages 33 and 41).

Slice and serve cold veal with fresh peeled and sliced peaches or pears, fresh whole figs, or sliced melon.

Combine equal parts finely diced veal and finely diced Swiss cheese. Bind with mustard-mayonnaise. Use as sandwich or hors d'oeuvre spread.

Place slices of cold veal on a long serving platter. Arrange anchovy fillets, slivers of ripe olives, and pimiento strips in an attractive design over meat. Surround with cold cooked carrot slices and tiny boiled white onions. Coat meat and vegetables with aspic jelly (see page 204).

Chill until firm. Garnish platter with radish roses, wedges of hard-cooked egg, parsley sprigs, and whole ripe olives.

HUNGARIAN GOULASH

1 *tablespoon butter*
1 *onion, peeled and sliced*
2 *carrots, scraped and sliced*
2 *stalks diced celery*
1 *small green pepper, seeded and cut into thin strips*
1 *small clove garlic, crushed*
½ *teaspoon paprika*
1 *teaspoon tomato paste*

1 *teaspoon flour*
1¾ *cups clear chicken broth*
2 *cups diced cooked veal, cut into 2-inch-long, ½-inch-thick strips*
¼ *cup sour cream*
1 *small sweet pimiento, cut in strips*

Heat butter in a deep heavy saucepan. Add onion, carrots, celery, green pepper, and garlic. Cook over moderate heat for 5 minutes, stirring occasionally. Stir in paprika, tomato paste, and flour. Add broth slowly stirring to blend. Cover and simmer gently for ½ hour. Add veal, cover, and cook over low heat for 15 minutes. Remove meat. Strain the sauce, pressing vegetables through a sieve. Return meat and sauce to pan. Stir in sour cream and pimiento. Heat thoroughly (do not allow to boil). Serve over rice or noodles.
[4 *servings.*]

SPAGHETTI WITH QUICK ITALIAN TOMATO AND VEAL SAUCE

3 *tablespoons olive oil*
1 *clove garlic, minced*
6 *large tomatoes, chopped*
Salt
Freshly ground   } *to taste*
 black pepper
2 *to 3 dashes Tabasco sauce*
1 *cup diced cooked veal*

2 *to 3 tablespoons veal gravy (optional)*
2 *tablespoons tomato purée*
1 *1-lb. package thin spaghetti*
½ *lb. mozzarella cheese, cut into small cubes*
2 *tablespoons chopped parsley*

Heat the olive oil with the garlic. Add the tomatoes and cook over moderate heat until mixture is reduced to a thick sauce. Stir frequently and chop the tomatoes with a knife or the tip of a spatula as they cook. Season with salt, pepper, and Tabasco sauce. Add the veal, veal gravy, and tomato purée. Blend well and simmer over low heat while cooking spaghetti.

Cook spaghetti according to package directions. Drain, place in large serving bowl. Add sauce, mozzarella cheese, and parsley. Blend well and serve.
[4 *servings*.]

NOTE: The heat of the sauce and spaghetti will soften and heat the cheese.

VEAL WITH MUSHROOMS PAPRIKA

2 *cups cooked veal, cut into*   ¾ *cup sour cream*
 thin strips about 1½ inches   1 *teaspoon paprika, more if*
 long   *desired*
1 *cup thinly sliced mushrooms*   Salt ⎱
3 *tablespoons butter*   Pepper ⎰ *to taste*

Cook the veal and mushrooms in the butter until mushrooms are tender (about 5 minutes). Add the sour cream, paprika, salt, and pepper. Cook, stirring, over low heat until sauce is well heated (do not allow to boil).

Serve over flat noodles or rice.
[4 *servings*.]

VEAL AND TOMATO SLICES À LA SUISSE

6 *to* 8 *slices cooked veal*   4 *tablespoons butter*
Salt ⎫   1 *tablespoon lemon juice*
Freshly ground ⎬ *to taste*   ¼ *cup dry sherry*
 black pepper ⎭   6 *to* 8 *thin slices Swiss cheese*
6 *to* 8 *large fresh mushrooms,*
 thinly sliced lengthwise

Sprinkle veal slices with salt and pepper, pressing seasoning into meat. Place in shallow ovenproof dish. Sauté mushrooms in butter in saucepan over medium heat for 2 to 3 minutes. Add lemon juice. Cook, stirring gently, 1 to 2 minutes. Add sherry, bring to boil, and pour over meat slices. Cover meat and sauce with overlapping slices of cheese. Bake in preheated 350° oven until cheese is melted, sauce bubbly. [4 *servings.*]

VEAL MARENGO

3 *tablespoons butter*
24 *small mushrooms*
2 *cups diced cooked veal*
1 *tablespoon flour*
½ *cup dry white wine*
1 *cup chicken stock, canned or homemade* (*see page* 203)
3 *tablespoons tomato purée*

8 *to* 12 *very small boiled white onions*
Salt
Freshly ground black pepper } *to taste*
2 *tablespoons chopped parsley*
Boiled white rice

Heat butter in large skillet. Add mushrooms and sauté 3 to 4 minutes. Add veal and cook, stirring, for 1 to 2 minutes. Stir in flour. When flour is lightly browned, add wine and chicken stock and stir until smooth. Blend in tomato purée, add onions and seasoning. Cook, stirring frequently, until sauce is thick and smooth. Add chopped parsley. Stir to blend, and serve over freshly cooked white rice.
[4 *servings.*]

QUICK CURRY OF VEAL

3 *tablespoons butter*
1 *large onion, chopped*
2 *large tart apples, chopped*
3 *to* 4 *stalks celery, chopped*
2 *tablespoons curry powder*
1 *tablespoon flour*
½ *teaspoon salt*

1½ *cups chicken stock* (*see page* 203)
1 *tablespoon tomato paste*
1 *tablespoon currant jelly*
2 *cups diced cooked veal*
4 *tablespoons grated coconut*
Freshly cooked rice

Melt the butter in a heavy skillet. Add the onion, apples, and celery. Cook, stirring frequently, until apples are tender and onion is soft. Stir in curry powder, flour, and salt. Add remaining ingredients, with the exception of the rice, and cook over low heat, stirring constantly, until sauce thickens and meat is thoroughly heated. Serve over freshly cooked white rice. Have traditional curry accompaniments to pass at the table: chopped peanuts, Bombay duck, crumbled bacon, chopped green onion, chutney, and toasted coconut.

Poultry

Poultry

A CHICKEN IN EVERY POT is America's just due—but why not extend this to include cold fried, roasted, or baked chicken (or turkey or duck) in every refrigerator? Nothing could be easier to come home to: set it out at room temperature while you mix up a good potato salad or prepare a hot vegetable soufflé. Serve with chilled dry white wine, a cold glass of beer, or, if you have it and are in a festive mood, with a split, or two, of champagne.

TO STORE: Wrap roasted poultry or poultry pieces in foil. Refrigerate; use within two or three days. Or, remove meat from bone, wrap in foil, and refrigerate up to one week. Or, slice or dice meat, place in shallow foil containers, cover with gravy or sauce, and freeze until firm. Wrap containers in foil and store in freezer up to six weeks.

Cover and refrigerate sautéed chicken in gravy or sauce; use within one week or freeze as above.

Cover boiled poultry with its own cooking liquid. Refrigerate; use within one week. Wrap fried chicken pieces in foil. Refrigerate up to one week.

Reheat sliced roasted or baked chicken, duck, or turkey in sufficient sauce to cover meat; cook only until thoroughly heated. Reheat sautéed chicken in its own gravy or sauce in a covered skillet on top of the stove or in a moderate oven. Reheat boiled chicken in its own cooking liquid. Do not attempt to reheat fried chicken; it will become overcooked and tasteless. Simply bring cold pieces to room temperature, and serve. Flavor is masked if chicken is served when overchilled.

BITS AND PIECES

Add thin strips of cooked chicken, turkey, or duck to clear

chicken soup or broth, to any creamed or clear soup, to a chef's salad, or to a salad of rice.

Mix equal parts cold diced turkey or chicken with chopped celery and green pepper; quickly fork-stir into jellied chicken consommé or madrilene.

Bind ground or finely diced chicken or turkey with sour cream; season with a bit of curry powder, salt, and pepper. Spread on crisp crackers.

Combine equal parts sour cream and cream cheese; blend with finely diced duck. Season with Beau Monde seasoning. Use as stuffing for scooped-out tiny cherry tomatoes or for celery.

BACHELOR'S (OR EASY) CHICKEN SPREAD

Place ⅓ cup mayonnaise, ¼ cup dry sherry, and a cup of diced chicken in electric blender. Blend until smooth. Season with paprika, freshly ground black pepper, and salt.

ROASTED CHICKEN IN MARINARA SAUCE
WITH SPAGHETTI

6 *pieces of cold roast chicken (thighs, breasts, wings, legs, etc.)*	½ *cup chicken stock, canned or homemade*
1 *tablespoon olive oil*	½ *teaspoon basil*
1 *tablespoon butter*	½ *teaspoon oregano*
1 *medium onion, chopped*	1 *teaspoon salt*
1 *clove garlic, minced*	*Freshly ground black pepper, to taste*
4 *cups canned Italian-style tomatoes with basil*	1 *1-lb. package thin spaghetti*
3 *tablespoons tomato paste*	1 *cup grated Parmesan cheese*

Remove chicken pieces from refrigerator. Let stand at room temperature while preparing sauce. Heat the oil and butter in a large heavy saucepan. Add onion and garlic. Cook, stirring, over medium heat until onion is limp but not browned. Add tomatoes, tomato paste, chicken stock, and seasoning. Blend, turn heat to low, and allow sauce to simmer gently for about 40 minutes, stirring occasionally. Add chicken pieces and cook a final 20 minutes, or until chicken is thoroughly heated.

Cook spaghetti according to package directions for *al dente*. Drain and place on large platter. Place chicken pieces in center, cover with some of the sauce, and sprinkle with Parmesan cheese.

Serve any remaining sauce separately.

[2 *to* 3 *servings.*]

SCALLOPED CHICKEN

1 *small onion, finely chopped*
½ *small carrot, scraped and finely chopped*
5 *tablespoons butter*
1½ *cups chicken stock or broth, canned or homemade*
1 *bay leaf*
1 *sprig parsley*
2 *to* 3 *peppercorns*
3 *tablespoons flour*

1½ *cups milk*
2½ *cups diced cooked chicken*
¼ *cup diced pimiento*
¼ *cup sliced pitted black olives*
Salt ⎱ *to taste*
Pepper ⎰
2 *egg yolks, well beaten*
½ *cup buttered soft bread crumbs*

Sauté onion and carrot in 2 tablespoons of the butter until onion is limp. Add chicken stock, bay leaf, parsley, and peppercorns. Bring to boil, lower heat, and allow to simmer very gently for 30 minutes. Strain and set aside.

Heat remaining butter in a second saucepan. Add flour and stir to a smooth paste. Gradually add milk and strained chicken stock. Stir until smooth. Add chicken, pimiento, and olives. Cook, stirring frequently, only until sauce begins to thicken. Remove from heat, season to taste with salt and pep-

per. Cool slightly, then quickly stir in egg yolks. Blend well, transfer to 4 small baking dishes. Sprinkle with bread crumbs and bake in a preheated 350° oven until surface is lightly browned (15 to 20 minutes).
[4 *servings.*]

CHICKEN CHOW MEIN WITH SNOW PEAS

1 *package frozen snow peas*
2 *tablespoons vegetable oil*
½ *cup shredded Chinese cabbage*
½ *cup finely sliced celery*
4 *tablespoons soy sauce*
1 *teaspoon sugar*
¼ *teaspoon monosodium glutamate*
⅓ *cup clear chicken stock or broth*

½ *cup canned bean sprouts, well drained*
1 *cup finely shredded cooked chicken*
½ *cup thinly sliced water chestnuts*
1 *teaspoon cornstarch dissolved in 2 teaspoons water*
Freshly cooked white rice
Crisp Chinese noodles

Remove frozen snow peas from package. Break up frozen block. Set aside at room temperature for 5 minutes.

Heat the oil in a large heavy skillet. Add the cabbage and celery. Cook, stirring, for 2 minutes. Add snow peas and remaining ingredients except cornstarch. Cover and cook until snow peas are crisp-tender.

Stir in cornstarch and cook, stirring, until sauce thickens.

Serve over freshly cooked white rice. Sprinkle each serving with crisp Chinese noodles.
[4 *servings.*]

CHICKEN ALMOND HASH

2 *tablespoons butter*
2 *tablespoons flour*
1 *cup chicken stock or broth, canned or homemade (see page* 203)
1 *cup light cream*
1½ *cups diced cooked chicken*

½ *cup slivered toasted almonds*
½ *cup sliced "sautéed in butter" mushrooms*
Salt ⎫
Pepper ⎭ *to taste*
Toast points

Melt butter in a heavy saucepan. Stir in flour. When mixture is smooth, slowly add stock, stirring it into the flour and butter as it is added. When this is blended, add the cream. Cook, stirring, over low heat until sauce thickens. Do not allow to boil. Add the chicken, almonds, and mushrooms, season with salt and pepper. Cook only until thoroughly heated. Serve over toast points.
[4 *servings.*]

TEN-MINUTE CREAMED CHICKEN AND NOODLES

1 *3-oz. package French Triple Crème Cheese, Swedish Hable Crème, Chantilly, or American cream cheese*
1 *cup cream*
20 *to* 24 *julienne strips cooked chicken, mixed white and dark meat*

1 *small can "sautéed in butter" sliced or diced mushrooms*
Salt ⎫
Pepper ⎭ *to taste*
1 *1-lb. package flat noodles*
2 *tablespoons finely chopped parsley*

Crumble cheese, combine with cream, chicken, and mushrooms. Season with salt and pepper. Place over very low heat and cook, stirring frequently, only until thoroughly hot. Do not allow to boil. (Do not overcook; if noodles are not ready, remove from stove, then reheat.)

Cook noodles according to package directions. Drain, place in large serving bowl. Add chicken sauce and parsley. Blend and serve.
[4 *servings.*]

SOUTHERN CHICKEN SALAD

3 cups finely diced or minced cold cooked chicken
1 cup finely diced celery
1 small onion, minced
1 medium green pepper, minced, all seeds and fiber removed
½ cup finely minced sweet pickle
2 hard-cooked eggs, finely chopped
¾ cup mayonnaise, homemade (see page 223), or ¾ cup commercial mayonnaise mixed with 1 tablespoon lemon juice
Salt
Pepper } to taste

Combine all ingredients in large mixing bowl. Blend well, cover, and refrigerate for 2 hours or more before serving.

Serve as salad or use as sandwich spread.

[6 to 8 servings as salad.]

OLD-FASHIONED CHICKEN À LA KING

4 tablespoons butter
4 tablespoons flour
1 cup chicken stock or broth (see page 203)
1 cup light cream
2 egg yolks, lightly beaten
1 small can "sautéed in butter" mushrooms
1 pimiento half, cut into thin strips
¾ teaspoon salt
¼ teaspoon pepper
2 tablespoons cognac (or other good brandy if preferred) or sherry
2½ to 3 cups diced cooked chicken
½ cup slivered toasted almonds, and/or ½ cup slivered pitted black olives (both optional)

Melt the butter in a large heavy saucepan. Stir in the flour. When mixture is smooth, add the stock, stirring it into the flour mixture as it is added. Add cream, blend, and cook, stirring, until sauce thickens. Do not allow to boil. Stir a tablespoon of the hot sauce into the egg yolks and add them to rest of sauce. Add remaining ingredients and cook, stirring, until thoroughly heated.

Serve over toast points or in heated patty shells.

[4 to 6 servings.]

EASY CHICKEN CURRY

1½ cups flaked or shredded
coconut
2 cups milk
¼ cup chopped shallots
3 tablespoons butter
1 tablespoon curry powder
½ teaspoon salt

3 tablespoons flour
1½ cups clear chicken stock or
broth, canned or homemade
(see page 203)
2 tablespoons dry sherry
2½ cups diced cooked chicken
Cooked white rice

Place coconut and milk in saucepan over low heat. Cook, stirring, until mixture foams (about 2 minutes). Remove from heat and strain through a fine sieve. Set coconut milk aside. Spread sieved coconut out on a baking sheet, place in 300° oven until lightly browned. Stir now and then with a fork. Set aside.

Sauté the shallots in the butter in a large saucepan. When these are limp, stir in the curry powder, salt and flour. Slowly add the prepared coconut milk, blend, and add chicken stock. Cook, stirring, until sauce is thick and smooth. Add sherry and chicken. Stir until chicken is heated. Serve over cooked rice. Sprinkle toasted coconut over each serving.
[4 servings.]

QUICK CHICKEN ENCHILADAS

1 small onion, chopped
1 small clove garlic, minced
2 tablespoons vegetable oil
1 medium can chili sauce,
without beans
16 tortillas, frozen or fresh
from Mexican grocery

1 cup shredded cooked
chicken
1 cup shredded Boston lettuce
1 cup shredded American or
Swiss cheese
½ cup chopped onion

Sauté onion and garlic in oil in heavy skillet until limp but not browned. Add chili sauce and cook, stirring frequently, until thoroughly heated. Remove from heat.

Dip each tortilla briefly in the hot sauce. Place some of the chicken and lettuce on each, roll up, and place in single layer on long ovenproof platter. Pour remaining sauce over surface. Place platter in preheated 400° oven for 5 minutes. Remove. Sprinkle cheese and onion over surface. Serve at once. [4 *servings*.]

CHICKEN CAPILOTADE WITH SAUCE CHASSEUR
(Chicken with Hunter's Sauce)

8 *to* 12 *thick slices of cooked chicken, white and dark meat*
½ *cup chopped mushrooms*
2 *tablespoons chopped shallots*
3 *tablespoons butter*
1 *teaspoon flour*
½ *cup white wine*

1 *cup chicken stock or broth, canned or homemade* (*see page* 203)
1 *teaspoon tomato purée*
¼ *teaspoon salt*
⅛ *teaspoon freshly ground black pepper*

Place chicken slices in an attractive, fairly deep ovenproof dish—one that may be brought to the table.

Sauté mushrooms and shallots in butter for 5 minutes. Remove them with a slotted spoon. Place over chicken.

Add flour to the butter remaining in the pan, blend, and add the wine. Stir until smooth. Add remaining ingredients and cook, stirring, until thick.

Pour sauce over chicken, mushrooms, and shallots. Place in preheated 350° oven until sauce is bubbly, chicken hot (about 10 minutes). Serve from dish.
[4 *to* 6 *servings*.]

TURKEY-APPLE SALAD

1 *cup diced cooked turkey*
½ *cup chopped raw mushrooms*
¼ *cup diced green pepper*
1 *tablespoon minced onion*
¼ *cup turkey or chicken stock,*
  canned or homemade
  (*see page* 203)
½ *teaspoon salt*

¼ *teaspoon freshly ground*
  black pepper
⅛ *teaspoon Beau Monde*
  seasoning

6 *large apples*
Turkey or chicken stock
Endive
Mayonnaise

Combine turkey, mushrooms, green pepper, onion, stock, and seasoning. Blend well.

Core apples and remove some of the fruit, leaving thick apple shells. Pare the top third of the skins.

Place apples in baking dish and fill centers with turkey mixture. Cover bottom of dish with about ½ inch of stock. Cover dish and bake apples in a preheated 375° oven until they are tender but not broken. Baste several times while baking.

Remove apples from stock and refrigerate until well chilled. Place on a bed of chopped endive, and garnish with mayonnaise.

[6 *servings.*]

COLD CHICKEN WITH MAYONNAISE COLLÉE

8 *substantial pieces of cooked chicken* (*thighs, breasts, legs, etc.*)

MAYONNAISE COLLÉE

2 *tablespoons gelatin*
¼ *cup cold water*
¼ *cup dry white wine*
2 *cups mayonnaise*
  (*see page* 223)

¼ *teaspoon curry powder*
  (*optional*)
Ripe olive slivers
Pimiento strips

Remove skin from chicken. Place on serving platter and cover with plastic wrap. Refrigerate while preparing mayonnaise collée.

Sprinkle gelatin over cold water in top of double boiler. Place over simmering water, stir until gelatin is dissolved. Remove from heat, stir in wine, and blend into mayonnaise. Add curry powder if desired. Spread mixture over chicken pieces, covering them completely. Arrange olive slivers and pimiento strips, in attractive design, over each piece of meat. Refrigerate one hour or longer or until ready to serve.

[4 *servings as an entree, 8 as part of a cold buffet supper.*]

HOT CHICKEN MOUSSE
WITH CREAMED VEGETABLES

3 *cups diced cooked chicken*
1 *small can "sautéed in butter"*
  mushrooms, chopped
1 *cup thick cream sauce*
  (*see page* 207)
¼ *cup dry sherry*
2 *tablespoons minced parsley*

1 *tablespoon minced green*
  onion
8 *eggs, lightly beaten*
Salt ⎫
Pepper ⎭ *to taste*
Creamed vegetables
  (*see page* 90)

Combine chicken, mushrooms, cream sauce, sherry, parsley, and onion, blend, and add eggs. Season with salt and pepper. Pour into lightly greased ring mold. Place in larger pan of hot water. Bake in preheated 375° oven until firm (30 to 40 minutes). Unmold onto serving platter, fill center of mousse with hot creamed vegetables.

[6 *servings.*]

CHICKEN EN BROCHETTE

1 *tablespoon soy sauce*
½ *cup sherry*
24 *cubes of cooked chicken,*
  each about 1½ *x* 1 *inch*
8 *slices thick smoked bacon*

24 *medium mushrooms*
2 *eggs, lightly beaten with* 1
  tablespoon vegetable oil
1½ *cups fine dry bread crumbs*

Combine soy sauce and sherry, pour over chicken cubes. Set aside for 30 minutes.

Cut each bacon slice into 3 pieces. Cook over low heat in heavy skillet for 5 minutes. Drain.

Place 3 cubes of chicken, 3 pieces of bacon, and 3 mushrooms on each of 8 small skewers.

Dip each prepared skewer in beaten eggs, then roll in bread crumbs. Arrange on rack over shallow roasting pan so that ends of skewers rest on edge of pan. Place under medium broiler heat until lightly browned. Turn them several times so that they brown on all sides.

[4 *servings.*]

TURKEY HASH

2 *tablespoons butter*
¾ *cup finely diced celery*
¼ *cup finely diced green pepper*
½ *cup finely diced mushrooms*
2 *cups thin cream sauce made with turkey or chicken stock (see pages 71 and 203)*
2 *tablespoons stuffing from roasted turkey, crumbled*

2 *cups diced roasted turkey, white or dark meat free of all skin and gristle*
2 *tablespoons cognac or other fine brandy*
2 *tablespoons fine dry bread crumbs*
2 *tablespoons melted butter*

Melt butter in a large saucepan. Add celery, green pepper, and mushrooms. Cook, stirring, over low heat for 5 minutes. Remove from heat. Add cream sauce and turkey stuffing. Stir, breaking up stuffing so that it becomes part of sauce. Add turkey and cognac, blend, and pour mixture into a shallow baking pan or into 6 individual baking dishes. Sprinkle with bread crumbs and melted butter. Bake in preheated 350° oven for 15 to 20 minutes, or until hash is thoroughly hot.

[6 *servings.*]

TURKEY AND BROCCOLI SUPREME

1 *package frozen broccoli*
8 *thin slices white meat of*
roasted turkey

2 *cups medium cream sauce*
made with turkey or chicken
stock (see pages 71 *and* 203)
½ *cup diced sharp cheese*

Cook broccoli according to package directions. Bring turkey slices to room temperature. Drain. Coarse chop. Place in long shallow baking dish. Cover with slices of turkey. Combine cream sauce and cheese; do not blend. Pour over turkey slices. Place under low broiler heat until surface is bubbly and lightly browned.
[4 *servings.*]

TURKEY SALAD

2 *cups diced white and dark*
meat of cooked turkey
1 *cup thinly sliced celery, with*
a few celery leaves
1 *tablespoon minced onion*
¾ *cup sliced or halved purple*
grapes, seeds removed
½ *cup toasted almonds*

¾ *cup mayonnaise, homemade*
(see page 223), *or* ¾ *cup*
commercial mayonnaise
blended with 1 *tablespoon*
lemon juice
¼ *teaspoon curry powder*
Lettuce leaves
Paprika

Combine turkey, celery, onion, grapes, and almonds.
Blend mayonnaise with curry powder. Add to turkey mixture and blend.
Refrigerate until salad is well chilled. Mound onto crisp lettuce leaves. Dust with paprika.
[4 *to* 6 *servings.*]

BRANDIED DUCK WITH HERBS

¼ cup butter
4 to 8 pieces of roasted duck
   (thighs, breasts, legs, wings,
   etc.)
2 tablespoons chopped parsley

2 tablespoons chopped chives
¼ teaspoon oregano
¼ cup fresh orange juice
¼ cup cognac or other fine
   brandy

Heat the butter in a large skillet. Add the duck, sprinkle with parsley, chives, and oregano. Cook over medium heat until duck is crisp on the underside. Turn, add the orange juice and brandy. Lower heat and simmer gently for 5 minutes. Transfer duck to heated serving plates, pour sauce over surface, and serve.
[4 servings.]

TURKEY OR DUCK SOUP

Carcass of roast turkey or duck
   plus any leftover scraps of
   meat and leftover stuffing
Cold water to cover, or part
   cold water, part chicken
   stock (about 4 quarts)
1 onion stuck with 2 cloves

2 ribs celery with leaves, cut up
2 leeks, sliced
3 to 4 sprigs fresh dill
1 parsnip, sliced
1 bay leaf
Salt
Pepper } to taste

Break up carcass and place with scraps and stuffing in large soup kettle. Cover with water or water and stock. Bring to boil. Lower heat and add remaining ingredients. Simmer very gently for 3½ to 4 hours. Strain. Serve over thick slices of crusty French bread.

Or, strain, refrigerate covered until fat rises to surface and congeals. Remove fat. Store covered in refrigerator; use within two to three days. Or freeze and store in freezer up to six weeks.

Use in place of chicken stock in sauces, gravies, etc.
[Makes about 3 quarts soup or stock.]

BAKED CHICKEN HASH

2 cups medium cream sauce   Salt ⎫
  (see page 207)   Pepper ⎬ to taste
2 cups diced cooked chicken,   2 tablespoons heavy cream
  white and dark meat   2 tablespoons grated
2 tablespoons sherry   Parmesan cheese
1 egg yolk, lightly beaten

Make cream sauce. Add chicken, sherry, and egg yolk. Blend well and season with salt and pepper to taste. Place in shallow baking dish. Combine cream and grated cheese and spread over surface. Place under medium broiler, heat until lightly browned. Serve from dish.

[4 servings.]

Fish

Fish

CAN LEFTOVER cooked fish be served a second time? The answer is yes of course—and no. Fish that has been poached in a simmering court bouillon retains its moist quality and flavor. After part has been "sauced" and served, the remaining portion can be refrigerated, to reappear the next day or even a day later in an entirely different guise—served hot or cold in any number of excellent ways long known to professional chefs.

Fish baked in wine or stock may be successfully substituted. Broiled fish—cooked but not overcooked with a small amount of oil or butter—may also be used, though the results may not be as satisfactory.

Fried fish: sorry, forget it.

For seafood croquettes and seafood soufflé not included in the following section see pages 210 and 217.

TO STORE: Remove skin and bones. Place in nonmetal airtight container or in sealed plastic bag. Use next day if possible; if not, no later than the day after. Or, place flaked fish in foil pan, cover with cooked sauce, wrap pan in foil, seal edges, and freeze. Store in freezer up to six weeks. Reheat in low oven or transfer to top of double boiler and reheat over simmering water.

BITS AND PIECES

Use leftover flaked fish to "extend" a seafood salad; shrimp with flaked cooked sole, halibut with lobster, crabmeat, and haddock, or what have you.

Bind flaked cooked fish with tartar sauce. Spread on buttered cocktail rye rounds or use to stuff small cherry tomatoes. Serve as hors d'oeuvre.

Add flaked fish to salad of mixed greens, or combine with minced green pepper and minced onion. Moisten with vinaigrette dressing and sprinkle over ripe tomato slices.

Add flaked fish to (canned) oyster bisque, creamed shrimp soup, cheese soup, or vegetable soup without meat.

Cover chunks of cold cooked fish with chili sauce. Place on lettuce-lined plates with wedges of hard-cooked eggs and fresh tomatoes, anchovy fillets, pickled beets or beans, and ripe or green olives. Serve as a seafood antipasto.

Add flaked cooked fish to a rich cream sauce. Spoon over just-cooked fresh asparagus on freshly made hot buttered toast —an easy but elegant luncheon.

AVOCADO FISH DIP

2 *large ripe avocados*   *Cayenne pepper* ⎱
1 *cup heavy cream*   *Salt*   ⎬ *to taste*
½ *cup dry white wine*   *Minced chives* ⎰
1 *teaspoon lemon juice*
1 *cup flaked cooked fish (sole,*
  halibut, haddock, etc.)

Cut each avocado in half, remove seed and skin. Mash fruit until smooth. Beat until light with rotary beater. Slowly beat in cream, add wine, lemon juice, and flaked fish. Blend well, season with cayenne pepper and salt. Pile into large serving bowl. Sprinkle surface with chives. Serve as dip with crisp crackers or melba toast rounds.
[*Makes about* 3 *cups dip.*]

ARTICHOKE AND FLAKED FISH COCKTAIL

1 *cup mayonnaise*
(*see page 223*)
¼ *cup chili sauce*
½ *teaspoon Worcestershire*
sauce
1 *tablespoon minced green*
onion

Salt, to taste
1½ *cups diced cooked*
(*canned, frozen, or fresh*)
artichoke hearts
1 *cup flaked cooked fish*
Lettuce

Combine mayonnaise with chili sauce, Worcestershire sauce, and green onion. Season with salt. Blend well and mix with artichoke hearts and fish. Serve in lettuce-lined cocktail cups.
[4 *to 6 servings.*]

AVOCADO-FISH SALAD

½ *cup salad oil*
¼ *cup white wine vinegar*
¼ *teaspoon salt*
¼ *teaspoon dry mustard*
⅛ *teaspoon pepper*
½ *clove garlic*

1½ *cups flaked cooked fish*
(*sole, trout, haddock, hali-*
but, etc.)
¼ *cup slivered ripe olives*
2 *large avocados*
Lemon juice
Romaine lettuce leaves

Combine first six ingredients. Blend well and pour over fish in nonmetal bowl. Cover and refrigerate for 2 to 3 hours. Remove garlic, drain, and add olive slivers.

Cut avocados in half, remove seeds, sprinkle with lemon juice. Spoon flaked fish mixture into cavities. Serve on crisp leaves of romaine.
[4 *servings.*]

MOLDED SEAFOOD SALAD

1 *envelope unflavored gelatin*
¾ *cup clam juice*
2 *tablespoons lemon juice*
2 *to* 3 *dashes Tabasco sauce*
¾ *cup mayonnaise*
¾ *cup finely diced celery*

¼ *cup finely diced green pepper*
¼ *cup finely chopped pimiento*
1 *cup flaked cooked fish* (*sole, trout, haddock, halibut, etc.*)
¼ *cup chopped cooked shrimp*
Lettuce

Sprinkle gelatin over clam juice in saucepan to soften. Place over low heat, stirring constantly, until gelatin is dissolved. Remove from heat and cool. Add lemon juice and Tabasco sauce. Stir slowly into mayonnaise and blend until smooth. Combine with remaining ingredients (except lettuce) and pour into small mold. Refrigerate until firm. Dip mold briefly in hot water. Unmold on crisp lettuce leaves. [4 *to* 6 *servings.*]

SEAFOOD SALAD

2 *cups flaked cooked fish*
½ *cup vinaigrette dressing*
1½ *cups chopped cooked shrimp*
½ *cup chopped celery*
1 *cup mayonnaise* (*see page* 223)

1 *hard-cooked egg, chopped*
2 *tablespoons chopped mixed pickles*
1 *tablespoon chopped green onion*
1 *chopped pimiento*
Lettuce

Combine flaked fish and vinaigrette dressing in nonmetal bowl. Refrigerate covered for 2 to 3 hours. Drain (reserve dressing). Combine fish with shrimp and celery.

Mix mayonnaise with 2 tablespoons of the reserved dressing. Blend in remaining ingredients (except lettuce) and add to fish and shrimp mixture. Serve from lettuce-lined bowl. [4 *to* 6 *servings.*]

SEAFOOD-RICE SALAD

¾ cup mayonnaise
1 tablespoon lemon juice
2 tablespoons chopped parsley
2 tablespoons capers, drained
2 tablespoons pimiento

¾ to 1 cup cold poached fish
(any combination of leftover
flaked fish or diced seafood)
1 cup cold cooked rice
Crisp lettuce leaves

Mix ½ cup of the mayonnaise with the lemon juice, parsley, capers, and pimiento. Combine with the fish and rice. Toss lightly to blend. Mound onto crisp lettuce leaves. Garnish each serving with remaining mayonnaise.
[4 servings.]

QUICK FISH LOAF

1½ cups cooked fish, flaked,
finely packed (sole, halibut,
haddock, etc.)
1 can cream of mushroom soup
1 small can "sautéed in butter"
chopped mushrooms
1 cup fine dry bread crumbs
3 eggs, slightly beaten

2 tablespoons cognac or dry
sherry
¼ teaspoon Beau Monde
seasoning
¼ teaspoon salt
¼ teaspoon freshly ground
black pepper
Cream sauce (see page 207)

Combine all ingredients except white sauce; blend well. Pack into a well-greased loaf pan (9 x 5 x 3). Bake in preheated 375° oven for 1 hour, or until surface is lightly browned. Remove from oven and let stand about 10 minutes before unmolding. Loosen from sides of pan and turn out onto platter. Serve with a rich white sauce.
[4 to 6 servings.]

CREAMED FISH WITH AVOCADO

2 tablespoons butter
2 tablespoons flour
2 cups milk
2 teaspoons sherry
¼ teaspoon salt
⅛ teaspoon pepper

1½ cups flaked cooked fish
    (sole, halibut, haddock, etc.)
2 medium avocados
1 egg yolk
Freshly made hot toast

Melt butter in a heavy saucepan, add flour, and blend well. Slowly add milk, stirring it into the flour-butter mixture as it is added. Cook, stirring, until smooth. Add sherry, salt, and pepper. When sauce thickens, remove from heat and add flaked fish.

Cut avocados in half, remove seeds, and peel. Cut into bite-size pieces and add to sauce. Stir in egg yolk. Return pan to low heat and cook, stirring gently to avoid breaking up avocado. Do not allow to boil. When mixture is steamy hot, spoon over toast and serve.

[2 servings.]

EASY SEAFOOD PIE

12 thin slices of white bread
Butter
1 cup flaked cooked fish (sole,
    trout, haddock, halibut, etc.)
1 cup finely chopped cooked
    shrimp

Salt
Freshly ground black pepper
1 lemon, cut in thin slices, peel
    and all seeds removed
2 cups milk
2 eggs, lightly beaten

Remove crust from bread slices and cut slices in half. Spread with soft butter. Cover the bottom of a shallow square baking dish with some of the bread, buttered side up. Cover bread with a layer of the flaked fish and shrimp. Sprinkle with salt and pepper and place a few slices of lemon over surface. Repeat until all ingredients are used, ending with buttered bread. Combine milk and eggs, blend, and pour over surface of "pie." Place in a 375° oven and bake until pie is firm and surface is lightly browned (25 to 30 minutes). [4 *to* 6 *servings.*]

CRÊPES FRUITS DE MER MORNAY
(Baked Crêpes with Flaked Creamed Fish and Cheese Sauce)

4 *tablespoons butter*
4 *tablespoons flour*
2 *cups milk*
¼ *cup dry white wine or sherry*
¼ *teaspoon salt*
1 *cup flaked cooked fish* (*sole, trout, haddock, halibut, etc.*)
¼ *cup slivered blanched almonds*
1 *small pimiento, chopped*
16 *small cooked crêpes* (*see page* 213)
2 *egg yolks*
½ *cup grated Parmesan cheese*

Melt butter in a heavy skillet. Stir in flour; when mixture is smooth, slowly add milk, blending it into the flour-butter mixture. Add wine (or sherry) and salt. Cook, stirring, over low heat until sauce thickens.

Remove from heat and add 1 cup of the sauce to the flaked fish. Add the almonds and pimiento and blend well.

Place a generous tablespoon of this filling on each cooked crêpe. Fold crêpes over and place in a single layer in a long shallow baking dish.

Add the egg yolks to the remaining sauce, blend, and cook, stirring, over low heat for about 5 minutes (until sauce is very hot and quite thick). Pour over crêpes in baking dish. Sprinkle surface with grated cheese and place dish in a preheated 375° oven until cheese topping is lightly browned. [4 *servings.*]

BROCCOLI-SALMON CASSEROLE

1 *package frozen broccoli*
2 *tablespoons butter*
2 *tablespoons flour*
1 *cup milk*
½ *teaspoon salt*

1 *tablespoon dry sherry*
1 *cup flaked cooked salmon, free of all skin and bones*
¼ *cup grated Parmesan cheese*
¼ *cup buttered bread crumbs*

Cook broccoli according to package directions. Drain and chop. Set aside. Melt butter in saucepan, stir in flour, and blend until smooth. Add milk, slowly stirring it into the flour-butter mixture. Add salt and sherry and cook, stirring, until sauce thickens. Remove from heat and add salmon.

Place broccoli in the bottom of a lightly buttered shallow baking dish. Pour salmon mixture over surface. Sprinkle with grated cheese and bread crumbs. Bake in a preheated 350° oven for 20 minutes, or until surface is lightly browned.
[2 *to 4 servings.*]

KEDGEREE

3 *cups flaked cooked fish, preferably salmon, but any fish may be used*
3 *cups cooked rice*
3 *hard-cooked eggs, chopped*
2 *tablespoons fresh lime juice*
1 *cup light cream*

¼ *teaspoon grated nutmeg*
¼ *teaspoon grated coriander*
¼ *teaspoon powdered ginger*
1 *teaspoon salt*
¼ *teaspoon pepper*
6 *tablespoons melted butter*

Combine fish, rice, and eggs, blend, and add lime juice, cream, seasonings, and 4 tablespoons of the melted butter. Transfer to a fairly deep baking dish and pour remaining butter over surface. Bake in a preheated 350° oven until mixture is firm and surface is lightly browned—about 30 minutes.
[6 *servings.*]

SEAFOOD TIMBALES

½ cup chopped mushrooms
¼ cup butter
1¼ cups soft bread crumbs
¼ cup clam juice
¾ cup flaked cooked fish (sole,
   trout, haddock, halibut, etc.)

¼ cup chopped cooked shrimp
6 eggs, well beaten
1 tablespoon dry sherry
⅛ teaspoon Beau Monde
   seasoning
¼ teaspoon salt

Sauté mushrooms in butter in a large saucepan for 3 to 4 minutes. Remove from heat and stir in the bread crumbs. Add remaining ingredients and blend well. Pour mixture into 8 individual buttered soufflé molds, filling them three-quarters full. Place in a pan of warm water and bake in a preheated 350° oven for 20 to 25 minutes or until firm. Unmold and serve with a rich cream or cheese sauce (see page 208). [*Makes 8 small timbales.*]

Vegetables

Vegetables

IT'S SAD BUT TRUE that many housewives in this country throw out leftover vegetables simply because they have been led to believe that "all the vitamins are lost by reheating." *Not so.*

Little loss need occur if the vegetable is quickly reheated in its own leftover cooking liquid, or if it is added with cooking liquid to hot sauce and cooked only until hot. Vitamins concentrated in the cooking liquid are absorbed by soft vegetables and are "plus" vitamins that would otherwise not be obtained.

If vegetables are cooked correctly in the first place—crisp-cooked quickly in a small quantity of water—and if uneaten portions are refrigerated without delay in airtight containers, leftovers will taste as good and be as good for you as when the vegetables were served the first time.

For Vegetable Soufflé see page 217.

For Vegetable Fritters see page 211.

For Vegetable Omelet see page 216.

TO STORE: Refrigerate, covered in cooking liquid; use within two or three days. Or, combine with desired sauce, cover and seal with foil, and freeze; use within six weeks.

LEFTOVER VEGETABLES EXTENDED

Add leftover cooked vegetables and leftover cooking liquid to freshly cooked vegetables 1 or 2 minutes before they are ready to take from the stove—green beans to diced carrots, stewed tomatoes to spinach, lima beans to kernel corn, kernel corn to cauliflower, and so on and so on.

Purée leftover cooked vegetables and leftover cooking liquid in electric blender. Add to cream sauce for chicken or seafood or—vegetables!

Reheat chopped or diced or whole small cooked vegetables in plenty of butter. Add lightly beaten egg and scramble. Serve on freshly made toast that has been spread with anchovy paste.

Make a medium cream sauce (see page 207). Add chopped or diced or whole small cooked vegetables. Serve over pasta, rice, toast, omelets, or scrambled eggs.

Reheat cooked vegetables in butter. Combine with freshly cooked and drained pasta or rice. Toss with a generous amount of grated cheese, chives, or parsley, or all three!

Purée cooked vegetables and their liquid in electric blender. Combine with equal part cottage cheese. Season with salt. Mash into mashed potatoes instead of butter. Or, scoop out centers of baked potatoes, mash potato with vegetable-cheese mixture, and fill shells.

VEGETABLES À LA PROVENÇALE

2 *strips bacon, chopped*
1 *small onion, chopped*
1 *clove garlic, minced*
2 *fresh tomatoes, chopped*
1½ *to 2 cups cooked vegetables*
　(chopped broccoli, chopped
　asparagus spears, chopped
spinach, small whole boiled onions, chopped eggplant, etc.)
¼ *cup vegetable cooking liquid* *(optional)*
Salt ⎫
Pepper ⎭ *to taste*

Cook the bacon in a saucepan until crisp. Remove and set aside. Add the onion, garlic, and tomatoes to the pan. Cook, chopping the tomatoes with the tip of a knife or a spatula, until mixture is reduced to a sauce. Add the vegetables and

vegetable cooking liquid. Continue cooking only until vegetables are heated. Season to taste with salt and pepper.
[4 *servings.*]

VEGETABLES AU GRATIN

3 *tablespoons butter*
3 *tablespoons flour*
1½ *cups milk*
½ *teaspoon salt*
2 *tablespoons dry sherry*
   (optional)
½ *cup mild soft cheddar*
   cheese, crumbled

1 *egg yolk, slightly beaten*
1½ *to 2 cups cooked vegetables*
   (chopped cauliflower or
   broccoli, well-drained
   chopped spinach, green
   beans or lima beans, etc.)
Fine dry bread crumbs
Paprika

Melt the butter in a saucepan, stir in flour. When mixture is smooth, slowly add milk, stirring it into the flour and butter as it is added. Cook, stirring, over low heat until sauce thickens. Add salt, sherry, and cheese. Stir until cheese is melted. Add a little of the hot sauce to the egg yolk, blend, and stir egg mixture into the sauce.

Add vegetables and transfer mixture to a shallow baking pan. Sprinkle with bread crumbs and paprika. Bake in a preheated 375° oven until sauce is bubbly hot and surface is lightly browned.
[4 *servings.*]

VEGETABLE PUDDING

4 *tablespoons butter*
4 *tablespoons flour*
1 *cup milk*
2 *cups cooked vegetables*
   (chopped broccoli or cauli-
   flower, drained chopped

   spinach, lima beans, green
   beans, kernel corn, etc.)
1 *tablespoon lemon juice*
½ *teaspoon salt*
⅛ *teaspoon nutmeg*
3 *eggs, well beaten*

Melt the butter in a saucepan. Blend in the flour. Add the milk slowly, stirring it into the flour-butter mixture as it is

added. Cook, stirring, until sauce thickens. Remove from heat and add remaining ingredients, blend, and pour into a 1½-quart baking dish. Bake in a preheated 350° oven until firm—about 25 minutes.
[6 *servings.*]

PURÉE OF VEGETABLES

1 *cup cooked vegetables (peas, lima beans, artichoke hearts, mushrooms)*

2 *to 3 tablespoons butter, room temperature*
Salt, to taste

Purée vegetables in electric blender or force through a sieve. Mix with sufficient butter to obtain the consistency of mashed potatoes. Heat in saucepan over very low heat. Season with salt and serve immediately.

Or, spoon mounds of the purée on cooked (canned or fresh) artichoke bottoms, large sautéed-in-butter mushroom caps, small rounds of fried-in-butter toast, or small sautéed-in-butter tomato slices. Place in a preheated 350° oven for a few minutes just before serving.

CREAMED VEGETABLES

2 *cups cooked vegetables (chopped or minced carrots, broccoli, spinach, asparagus)*
2 *tablespoons butter*

¼ *cup heavy cream*
Salt ⎫
Pepper ⎭ *to taste*

Combine ingredients in saucepan, place over low heat, and cook, stirring, until hot. Do not allow to boil. Serve at once.
[4 *servings.*]

NOTE: Substitute sour cream for the heavy cream if desired.

VEGETABLES WITH ROQUEFORT CREAM SAUCE

2 *cups cooked vegetables*
(chopped broccoli, or aspar-
agus, whole boiled onions,
lima beans, peas, etc.)
¼ *cup leftover liquid from*
cooked vegetables

1 *tablespoon butter*
2 *tablespoons Roquefort*
cheese, crumbled
½ *cup sour cream*
1 *tablespoon minced chives*

Reheat vegetables in cooking liquid and butter. Combine Roquefort cheese, sour cream, and chives. Add to hot vegetables. Cook a final 1 to 2 minutes. Serve at once.
[4 *to* 6 *servings.*]

Soups

CREAM OF VEGETABLE SOUP

2 cups clear broth or stock (chicken or beef) or clam juice
2 tablespoons butter
1 tablespoon flour
½ teaspoon salt
¼ teaspoon pepper

1 cup cooked vegetables with cooking liquid (carrots, peas, lima beans, broccoli, spinach, cauliflower, etc.—any combination of 2 or more leftover vegetables)
2 cups light cream

Place all ingredients except cream in electric blender. Blend until smooth. Pour into saucepan. Add cream. Cook over low heat until steamy hot. (Do not allow to boil.)

Serve hot, or chill and serve cold. Garnish, if desired, with chopped chives, paprika, parsley, croutons, or grated cheese. [4 to 6 servings.]

NOTE: Milk may be used instead of stock.

POTAGE ST. GERMAIN
(Green Pea Soup)

2 cups chicken stock or broth
1 cup cooked green peas
1 small onion, chopped
1 small carrot, scraped and sliced
½ teaspoon sugar
1 tablespoon butter

1 cup light cream
Salt
Freshly ground black pepper } to taste
Chopped fresh mint leaves
Butter-fried croutons

Place stock, peas, onion, and carrot in electric blender. Blend until smooth. Pour into saucepan, add sugar, butter, and cream. Cook, stirring, over low heat until steamy hot. (Do

not allow to boil.) Season with salt and pepper. Stir in mint
leaves. Ladle into soup tureen and float croutons on surface.
[4 *to* 6 *servings.*]

JELLIED SUMMER VEGETABLE SOUP

2 *envelopes unflavored gelatin*
¼ *cup liquid from leftover*
  vegetables (*or water*)
1 *cup boiling hot stock,*
  canned or homemade
  (*see page* 202)
1 *cup cold stock*

½ *cup dry sherry*
1 *tablespoon lemon juice*
½ *cup chopped cooked carrots*
½ *cup cooked green peas*
¼ *cup chopped celery*
2 *tablespoons chopped chives*
Chopped parsley

Sprinkle gelatin over vegetable liquid to soften. Combine
with boiling hot stock and stir until gelatin has dissolved. Add
cold stock, sherry, and lemon juice. Refrigerate until mixture
is of egg-white consistency. Stir in remaining ingredients (except parsley) and transfer to a shallow wet pan. Refrigerate.
When mixture is firm, scramble coarsely with a fork. Spoon
into chilled bouillon cups. Sprinkle with chopped parsley and
serve.
[4 *to* 6 *servings.*]

BORSCHT

3 *cups clear chicken stock,*
  canned or homemade
  (*see page* 203)
1 *cup chopped cooked beets*
1 *small onion, chopped*
½ *cup tomato purée*
1 *tablespoon lemon juice*

½ *teaspoon sugar*
Salt
Freshly ground ⎫
  black pepper ⎬ *to taste*
2 *egg yolks, lightly beaten* ⎭
Sour cream

Combine 1 cup of the stock with remaining ingredients
(except egg yolks and sour cream) in electric blender. Blend
until smooth, pour into saucepan, add remaining stock, and
heat thoroughly. Stir 1 to 2 tablespoons of the hot soup into

the egg yolks. Stir egg yolk mixture into soup. Remove from heat immediately. Serve hot or cold with a generous tablespoon of sour cream over each serving.

[4 *servings.*]

CREAM OF TOMATO SOUP

1½ *cups stewed tomatoes*
1 *rib celery, cut in 2 or 3 pieces*
3 *to 4 scallions*
½ *cup milk*
1 *teaspoon flour*

½ *teaspoon sugar*
½ *teaspoon salt*
¼ *teaspoon white pepper*
1 *cup light cream*
2 *tablespoons dry sherry*

Place tomatoes, celery, scallions, milk, and flour in electric blender. Blend until smooth. Pour into saucepan, add remaining ingredients. Place over low heat. Blend and stir until steamy hot. (Do not allow to boil.)

[2 *to 4 servings.*]

Leftover Vegetables and Salads

THIS AND THAT

Almost any vegetable that was crisp-cooked in the first place (as it should be) goes well in a salad of mixed greens. Blend leftover cooking liquid and fresh lemon juice with mayonnaise for a perfect dressing.

Cover leftover vegetables with garlicky French dressing in nonmetal container. Refrigerate covered overnight. Drain and add to any combination of crisp greens. Toss with no more of the drained dressing than necessary to coat greens lightly.

Marinate crisp-cooked vegetables as above, drain, and serve with any good spicy dip. Serve with cocktails.

VEGETABLE SALAD MOLD

2 *envelopes unflavored gelatin*
¼ *cup cold leftover liquid from vegetables (or water)*
2 *cups boiling hot clear chicken stock or consommé, canned or homemade (see page* 203)
1 *cup leftover chopped asparagus, green beans, or broccoli*
¼ *cup chopped celery*
¼ *cup chopped pimiento*
2 *tablespoons minced green onion*
2 *tablespoons mayonnaise*
½ *teaspoon salt*
1 *tablespoon lemon juice*
½ *cup heavy cream*
Crisp lettuce leaves

Sprinkle gelatin over cold liquid to soften. Add boiling consommé or stock, stir until gelatin is blended. Refrigerate until mixture is of egg-white consistency. Combine with remaining ingredients (except cream and lettuce).

Whip cream until stiff and fold into gelatin mixture. Pour into wet mold and refrigerate until firm. Dip mold briefly

into hot water. Use table knife to loosen salad from mold, invert, and turn out onto lettuce-lined platter.
[4 *to* 6 *servings.*]

BROCCOLI AND BELGIAN ENDIVE SALAD WITH ROQUEFORT DRESSING

¼ *cup mayonnaise*
1 *teaspoon lemon juice*
3 *tablespoons heavy cream*
2 *tablespoons crumbled*
 Roquefort cheese

1 *cup coarsely chopped cooked*
 broccoli
2 *heads of endive, trimmed and*
 coarsely chopped
Lettuce leaves

Blend mayonnaise with lemon juice, cream, and crumbled cheese. Combine with broccoli and endive. Toss to blend. Serve on crisp lettuce leaves.
[4 *servings.*]

CAULIFLOWER SALAD

½ *cup mayonnaise*
1 *tablespoon lemon juice*
1 *tablespoon capers*
2 *tablespoons minced chives*

¼ *cup chopped black olives*
2 *cups cold cooked cauliflower*
 flowerets
Romaine lettuce

Blend mayonnaise with lemon juice, capers, and chives. Combine with olives and cauliflower. Toss to blend. Serve from salad bowl lined with romaine lettuce leaves.
[4 *servings.*]

GREEN BEAN SALAD

2 *cups cold cooked green*
 beans
1 *large red onion, chopped*
1 *teaspoon sugar*
2 *teaspoons cider vinegar*

¼ *cup salad oil*
Salt
Freshly ground
 black pepper
Lettuce
} *to taste*

Combine beans and onion. Mix sugar with vinegar, oil,

salt, and pepper. Pour over beans and onion, and blend. Pile into lettuce-lined salad bowl and serve.
[4 *servings.*]

BEET SALAD

Follow recipe for green bean salad. Substitute coarsely chopped beets for green beans.

SALAD OF RICE AND PICKLED BLACK-EYED PEAS

1 *cup cooked black-eyed peas*   1 *cup cold cooked rice*
½ *cup salad oil*   1 *small sweet red onion,*
2 *tablespoons wine vinegar*   *chopped*
1 *clove garlic*   *Freshly ground black pepper*
¼ *teaspoon salt*   *Lettuce*

Combine black-eyed peas with salad oil, vinegar, garlic, and salt. Cover and refrigerate for 8 hours or longer. Remove garlic and drain of all but about 1 tablespoon dressing. Add rice and onion, add pepper to taste. Serve well chilled from lettuce-lined bowl.
[4 *servings.*]

ASPARAGUS SALAD

⅓ *cup French dressing*   2 *tablespoons sour cream*
8 *to* 12 *cooked asparagus*   2 *to 4 anchovy fillets*
  spears   4 *to 6 jumbo black olives*
Lettuce leaves
1 *small tomato, cut into* 4
  wedges

Pour French dressing over asparagus. Cover and refrigerate in nonmetal bowl for 1 hour or longer. Drain and place in individual salad bowls lined with crisp lettuce leaves. Add tomato wedges. Spoon sour cream over asparagus. Garnish with anchovy fillets and black olives.
[4 *servings.*]

PEAS AND LETTUCE SALAD WITH HAM

1 *head Boston lettuce*
2 *cups cooked green peas*
½ *cup diced ham*
½ *cup pitted and sliced black olives*
2 *hard-cooked eggs*

¼ *cup salad oil*
2 *tablespoons white wine vinegar*
1 *teaspoon salt*
¼ *teaspoon freshly ground black pepper*

Tear lettuce into bite-size pieces. Wash, drain, and pat dry with paper toweling.

Combine with peas, ham, and olive slices. Place in salad bowl.

Mash egg yolks with olive oil and vinegar. Season with salt and pepper. Add to salad bowl. Toss ingredients until well blended. Chop egg whites and sprinkle over surface of salad.

[4 *to* 6 *servings.*]

Potatoes

Boiled Potatoes

IF YOU ARE EVEN the least enthusiastic of cook-ahead cooks, you will have boiled potatoes on hand. Cold and unadorned they are unappetizing, to say the least. But dress them in a good salad or heat them in any one of a dozen different ways, slice some cold leftover meat, and *voilà!* dinner is served.

TO STORE: Place dry potatoes in plastic bag or airtight container, or wrap in foil. Refrigerate; use within one week. Do not freeze.

TO REHEAT: Slice cold boiled potatoes, place in small amount of cooking oil or butter in heavy skillet. Cook over medium heat until slices are lightly browned on both sides. Season with salt.

Or, slice, place in single layer on greased foil. Dot with butter or sprinkle with oil, season with salt. Heat in 350° oven until lightly browned.

THIS AND THAT

Add small whole or quartered large potatoes to roasting pan about 45 minutes before meat is done and baste with drippings.

Or, coat potatoes with melted butter or cooking oil, place in shallow baking dish, season with salt and pepper. Reheat in 350° oven until potatoes are lightly browned.

Dice peeled potatoes, reheat in small amount of light cream or milk in top of double boiler over simmering water. When almost all liquid has been absorbed, season with butter, salt, and pepper. Sprinkle, if desired, with chopped parsley or chives.

Or, reheat, diced or sliced, in thin cream sauce (see page 207).

BAKED POTATO CASSEROLE

2 cups sliced boiled potatoes
1 cup diced Swiss cheese
2 medium-size sweet red
  onions, sliced and broken
  into rings
2 tablespoons butter

Salt
Freshly ground black pepper
1 cup sour cream
¼ cup fine dry bread crumbs
¼ cup melted butter

Arrange alternate layers of potatoes, cheese, and onions in well-buttered deep baking dish. Dot each layer with butter and sprinkle with salt and pepper. Pour sour cream over surface. Cover with bread crumbs and melted butter. Cover and bake in a preheated 375° oven for 25 minutes; uncover and bake a final 10 minutes.
[4 servings.]

SPANISH OMELET

Though this classic Spanish omelet is traditionally made with raw potatoes, we've found that boiled potatoes, if firm enough to dice without crumbling, substitute successfully. There's very little flavor difference in the final dish, and what's more, cooking time is shortened.

2 tablespoons olive oil—additional olive oil as needed
1 medium onion, finely diced
2 medium boiled potatoes,
  finely diced

½ teaspoon salt
½ teaspoon freshly ground
  black pepper
4 large or 5 medium eggs, well
  beaten

Heat oil in a heavy 10-inch skillet. Add onion. Cook, stirring, over medium heat until onion is translucent. Add potatoes. Continue cooking and stirring until onion is limp and potatoes well coated with oil and very hot. (Do not allow to brown.) Blend in salt and pepper, reduce heat to very low, and pour in eggs. Cook for 8 to 10 minutes, lifting omelet up as it sets to allow moist eggs to run under. When omelet is lightly browned on the bottom, gently loosen edges and underside with spatula. Invert plate over top of pan and turn out upside down on plate. Quickly wipe pan clean with a bit of absorbent paper soaked in olive oil. Then slide omelet back again, moist side down. Cook until firm and brown on second side.

[4 *servings.*]

CHÂTEAU POTATOES

2 *to* 3 *medium boiled potatoes*   *Salt*
2 *to* 3 *tablespoons butter*   *Chopped parsley*

Cut firm boiled potatoes in the shape of large olives. Sauté in butter over low heat until golden and thoroughly hot. Season with salt. Sprinkle with chopped parsley.

[4 *to* 6 *servings.*]

O'BRIEN POTATOES

4 *medium boiled potatoes, cut into small cubes*
1 *tablespoon butter*
1 *tablespoon oil*
1 *small onion, chopped*
½ *small green pepper, seeded and chopped*
2 *teaspoons butter*
½ *cup diced pimiento*
Salt ⎱
Pepper ⎰ *to taste*

Cook potatoes in butter and oil in heavy saucepan over medium heat, stirring until they are lightly browned on all sides.

In separate saucepan, sauté onion and green pepper in the 2 teaspoons butter until limp. Combine with potatoes. Add

pimiento and cook, stirring, a final 1 to 2 minutes. Season to taste with salt and pepper.
[*4 to 6 servings.*]

FARMER'S BREAKFAST

A country favorite up Vermont way "of a cold morning." You'll find it a city favorite too, especially with men.

8 *slices of bacon, chopped*	6 *eggs*
1 *small onion, chopped*	3 *tablespoons cream*
1 *small green pepper, seeded and chopped*	*Salt*
2 *small or* 1 *large boiled potato, chopped*	*Pepper* } *to taste*
	Paprika

Fry bacon in heavy 10-inch skillet until done but not over-crisp. Pour off all but 3 tablespoons of drippings. Add onion, green pepper, and potato. Cook, stirring, until vegetables are limp, potatoes lightly browned. Beat eggs with cream only until blended, season lightly with salt and pepper. Pour over bacon and vegetables. Cook over low heat, stirring occasionally, until eggs are set but still moist. Sprinkle with paprika.
[*4 servings.*]

FLEMISH SALAD

4 *medium boiled potatoes, peeled and cut in thick strips*	1 *tablespoon lemon juice*
1 *heart of chicory, torn into bite-size chunks*	1 *tablespoon salad oil*
	½ *teaspoon salt*
1 *large sweet red onion, sliced and broken into rings*	½ *teaspoon pepper*
	2 *jars (8 oz. each) herring in wine sauce*
2 *tablespoons mayonnaise*	*Chopped parsley*

Combine potatoes, chicory, and onion rings. Mix mayonnaise with lemon juice, salad oil, salt, and pepper. Add to potato mixture. Toss lightly to blend. Mound onto serving plates. Top with fillets of herring. Sprinkle with chopped parsley.

[4 *to* 6 *servings.*]

SALAD NIÇOISE

4 *medium boiled potatoes, peeled and sliced*

2 *tablespoons chopped chives*

4 *tablespoons vinaigrette dressing (see page 225) additional dressing as called for in recipe*

1 *package frozen string beans*

Lettuce

1 *small can flat anchovy fillets*

1 *small can tuna fish*

2 *medium tomatoes, cut into wedges*

1 *medium green pepper, seeded and cut into very thin strips*

1 *medium-size sweet red onion, cut into very thin slices, then rings*

Black olives

Salt, to taste

Peppercorns

Combine potatoes, chives, and 2 tablespoons of the vinaigrette dressing. Chill. Cook string beans according to package directions. Drain. Add remaining dressing. Chill.

At serving time arrange crisp lettuce leaves on individual salad plates. Place mounds of well-drained potatoes and string beans separately on lettuce. Top each with anchovy fillets. Add chunks of tuna, tomato wedges, green pepper strips, onion rings, and olives to each plate. Have salt, pepper mill, and carafe of dressing on the table.

[4 *to* 6 *servings.*]

POTATO AND APPLE SALAD

3 *medium boiled potatoes,*
peeled and diced
2 *medium-size crisp apples,*
cored and diced
4 *celery stalks, diced*
2 *tablespoons minced chives*

4 *tablespoons mayonnaise*
1 *tablespoon lemon juice*
1 *teaspoon salt*
½ *teaspoon freshly ground*
black pepper
Lettuce

Combine all ingredients (except lettuce). Blend well. Chill. Serve on crisp lettuce leaves.
[6 *servings.*]

SALAD A L'ARGENTEUIL

3 *medium boiled potatoes,*
peeled and diced
2 *tablespoons mayonnaise*
2 *tablespoons chopped chives*
½ *teaspoon salt*
1 *package frozen asparagus*

3 *tablespoons vinaigrette*
dressing (see page 225)
Lettuce
Thin strips of pimiento
2 *hard-cooked eggs, quartered*
Ripe olives

Mix potatoes with mayonnaise, chives, and salt. Chill. Cook asparagus according to package directions. Drain. Cover with vinaigrette dressing. Chill.

At serving time fill lettuce-lined glass salad bowl with potatoes. Arrange well-drained asparagus in wheel design over surface, lay strips of pimiento over asparagus, and place hard-cooked eggs and olives around edge of bowl.
[4 *to 6 servings.*]

INSALATA DI PATATE E ARAGOSTA
(Italian Potato and Lobster Salad)

In Italy you will find this dish and its many variations (shrimp substituted for lobster, no tomato but hearts of lettuce, etc.) served as an antipasto rather than a salad. We add it to our buffet supper table or serve it as the entree for a party luncheon.

4 *medium boiled potatoes, peeled and sliced*
2 *cups diced cooked lobster meat*
6 *anchovy fillets, chopped*
1 *tablespoon capers*
4 *tablespoons mayonnaise*
2 *tablespoons olive oil*

2 *tablespoons lemon juice*
½ *to 1 teaspoon salt*
½ *to 1 teaspoon freshly ground black pepper*
1 *small head romaine lettuce*
2 *medium tomatoes, cut into wedges*
12 *black olives*

Place potatoes, lobster, anchovy fillets, and capers in large salad bowl. Blend mayonnaise with olive oil, lemon juice, salt, and pepper. Add to potato-lobster mixture. Toss lightly to blend, taking care not to break potato slices. Tear romaine into bite-size pieces. Add to bowl. Again, blend lightly. Arrange tomato wedges and olives around edge of bowl.
[6 *to 8 servings.*]

MIKADO SALAD

2 *medium boiled potatoes, peeled and diced*
1 *cup chopped cooked shrimp*
¼ *cup chopped celery*

½ *cup mayonnaise*
1 *tablespoon soy sauce*
Salt, *to taste*
Lettuce

Combine potatoes with shrimp and celery. Mix mayonnaise with soy sauce. Blend into potato-shrimp mixture. Season with salt to taste. Refrigerate covered in nonmetal bowl until well chilled. Serve on crisp lettuce leaves.
[4 *to 6 servings.*]

POTATO AND CELERY ROOT SALAD

1 *small celery root*
Salt
Lemon juice
3 *to 4 medium boiled potatoes,*
  diced
3 *to 4 sprigs parsley, chopped*

½ *cup mayonnaise*

1 *teaspoon lemon juice*
1 *tablespoon hot prepared*
  mustard
Salt ⎫
Freshly ground ⎬ *to taste*
  black pepper ⎭
Watercress

Peel celery root and remove all dark spots. Dice into ½-inch cubes. Cook in boiling salted water with a few drops of lemon juice until crisp-tender (6 to 8 minutes). Drain, cool, and combine with cold diced potatoes and parsley. Mix mayonnaise with lemon juice and mustard. Combine with potato-celery root mixture. Season to taste with salt and pepper. Chill. Serve garnished with chopped watercress.
[4 *to 6 servings.*]

CONTINENTAL POTATO SALAD

4 *medium boiled potatoes,*
  peeled and diced
4 *stalks celery, diced*
¼ *lb. Swiss cheese, diced*
6 *artichoke hearts, halved*
  (canned, fresh, frozen)
6 *to 8 fresh mushrooms, sliced*
1 *tablespoon capers*

2 *hard-cooked eggs, chopped*
1 *tablespoon wine vinegar*
3 *tablespoons salad oil*
1 *teaspoon salt*
½ *teaspoon cracked black*
  peppercorns
1 *teaspoon sugar*
Romaine lettuce

Place first seven ingredients in mixing bowl. Combine vinegar, oil, salt, pepper, and sugar. Beat with wire whisk until light and frothy. Pour over potato salad and toss lightly to blend. Serve in glass salad bowl lined with leaves of romaine.
[6 *to 8 servings.*]

Mashed Potatoes

CONTRARY TO POPULAR OPINION, mashed potatoes can indeed be served a second time—either mashed again with more butter and cream (and to heck with that diet) or shaped into rich little patties and butter fried.

They make an excellent base for delicious fritters, and they may be used for duchess potatoes par excellence. If the purists frown at such short-cut methods, very few will complain about the final results.

TO STORE: Place in airtight container or in a bowl covered and sealed with foil or plastic wrap. Refrigerate; use within two or three days. Or, shape into small flat patties. Place, not touching, on flat tray and freeze until firm. Stack with wax paper between each patty, wrap stack in foil, and store in freezer. Use within one month.

TO REHEAT: Bring cold mashed potatoes to room temperature. Heat a small amount of butter and milk in a heavy saucepan. Add potatoes. Beat and remash with wooden spoon over low heat until smooth and hot. Use about ¼ cup milk or light cream and 1 teaspoon butter for each cup of potatoes previously mashed with milk or cream and butter.

THIS AND THAT

Fry frozen patties in a small amount of butter in a heavy skillet over medium heat until they are thoroughly heated and lightly browned on both sides.

POTATOES CHANTILLY

½ cup milk
1 tablespoon butter
3 cups leftover mashed
potatoes

Salt ⎫
Pepper ⎭ to taste
⅓ cup heavy cream
¼ cup grated cheese

Heat milk with butter in large saucepan. Add potatoes. Blend, over low heat, until smooth. Transfer to well-buttered baking dish and sprinkle with salt and pepper. Beat cream until stiff. Spread evenly over potatoes. Sprinkle with grated cheese. Bake at 350° until cheese is melted, topping lightly browned.

[4 to 6 servings.]

POTATO SOUFFLÉ

½ cup light cream
1 tablespoon butter
2 cups leftover mashed
potatoes
½ to 1 teaspoon salt

Dash of nutmeg
¼ to ½ teaspoon white pepper
2 tablespoons grated Parmesan
cheese
4 eggs, separated

Heat the cream with butter in large saucepan over medium heat. Stir in the potatoes and cook, stirring, until mixture is smooth and hot. Add seasoning (amount depends on seasoning of leftover mashed potatoes) and cheese and then beat in the egg yolks one at a time, beating well after each addition. Beat egg whites until stiff but not dry. Fold into potato mixture. Transfer to well-buttered deep baking dish. Bake at 350° until soufflé is well puffed and lightly browned (25 to 30 minutes).

[4 to 6 servings.]

POTATO DUMPLINGS WITH PORK

½ cup diced cooked pork
1 small onion, coarsely
    chopped
Cooking oil or diced fat from
    pork
1½ cups leftover mashed
    potatoes

1 large or 2 small eggs
½ teaspoon salt
½ teaspoon pepper
2 to 2½ cups flour
4 to 5 beef bouillon cubes
Water
Cream sauce

Fry pork with onion in small amount of cooking oil (or fat from pork roast) until onion is limp. Set aside. In mixing bowl, combine potatoes, eggs, salt, pepper, and 1 cup of the flour and blend until smooth. Turn out onto a lightly floured board. Knead in enough of the remaining flour to form a light, smooth dough. Form dough into small balls. Make a hole in the center of each and stuff with a small amount of the pork mixture, close, and roll each ball in flour.

Mix bouillon cubes with 1 cup of boiling water. Add about 6 cups of water and bring to boil in large pot. Add potato balls a few at a time. Cook 20 to 25 minutes. Remove with slotted spoon. Serve hot with cream sauce (see page 207). [4 to 6 servings.]

Rice

Rice

It's no exaggeration to say that with two cups of leftover cooked rice plus whatever else can be found in the refrigerator, any versatile cook can produce a meal far beyond the sum of its parts—though it goes without saying that the final result depends not only on how the rice was first cooked but also very much on what type of rice was used.

Cooked rice for leftover planning should be fluffy and dry—but *not* dried out.

First choice for the gourmet is the short-grain rice from the Piedmont region of Italy. When cooked, it is soft, creamy, and extremely flavorful, yet the fat little grains are separate and will remain so when reheated or used as an ingredient in any improvised dish. This kind of rice is seldom sold in supermarkets. You will, however, find it on the shelves of most Italian grocery stores, and it may be purchased or ordered from the delicacy department of many fine shops.

Long-grain rice is the next best choice. But be sure to get *plain* Carolina rice. Precooked rice or converted rice may of course be used, but these are poor substitutes.

TO STORE: Place well-drained rice in an airtight container or a bowl covered and sealed with foil or plastic wrap. Refrigerate; use within one week.

TO REHEAT: Put cold boiled rice in a colander. Cover colander with a clean kitchen towel or napkin that has been rung out in hot water. Place over a pot containing about 2 inches of barely simmering water. (Do not allow water to touch rice.) Let the rice steam until well heated.

RICE SALAD À LA FRANÇAISE

1 *large tomato*
2 *cups cold boiled rice*
1 *small sweet red onion,*
   chopped
2 *to 3 stalks celery, chopped*
4 *to 6 large fresh mushrooms,*
   thinly sliced lengthwise
2 *thin slices cold boiled ham*
   cut in julienne strips

2 *tablespoons wine vinegar*
5 *to 6 tablespoons salad oil*
1 *teaspoon salt*
½ *teaspoon freshly ground*
   black pepper
⅛ *teaspoon curry powder*
Lettuce

Cut tomato in half and gently squeeze each half to remove seeds and juice. Cut into small pieces. Combine with rice, onion, celery, mushrooms, and ham. Mix vinegar with salad oil and seasonings. Blend well with wire whisk. Pour over rice mixture, toss lightly. Serve on crisp lettuce leaves. [4 *to 6 servings.*]

QUICK RICE AND BEANS

2 *slices of thick smoked bacon,*
   diced
1 *medium-size sweet red onion,*
   diced
1 *small green pepper, diced,*
   free of all seeds and fiber
1 *small clove garlic, minced*
1 *medium can Italian-style*
   tomatoes with basil

1 *medium can kidney beans*
1 *teaspoon salt*
¼ *teaspoon freshly ground*
   black pepper
⅛ *teaspoon rosemary*
⅛ *teaspoon oregano*
3 *cups cold boiled rice*
⅓ *cup grated Parmesan cheese*

Cook the bacon in a large heavy skillet over medium heat until done but not overcrisp. Remove with slotted spoon and set aside. Pour all but about 1 tablespoon of bacon fat from the skillet. Add the onion, green pepper, and garlic, sauté until vegetables are limp but not browned. Return the diced cooked bacon to the skillet. Add tomatoes, beans, and seasonings.

Cover and allow to simmer gently over low heat for about 20 minutes. Add the rice, fork-stir to blend, and cook a final 2 minutes. Stir in the cheese and serve.

[6 *servings.*]

BLACK BEANS AND RICE

1 *cup black beans*
1 *quart water, additional water if needed*
¼ *lb. salt pork, diced*
1 *clove garlic, minced*
1 *medium onion, chopped*
1 *teaspoon salt*
½ *teaspoon freshly ground black pepper*
1 *bay leaf*
⅛ *teaspoon thyme*
⅛ *teaspoon oregano*
3 *cups cold boiled rice*
¼ *cup chopped green onion*

Soak beans overnight in the 1 quart of water, or place beans in water, bring to full boil, boil for 10 minutes, and then let beans soak, covered, for 1 hour.

Place beans and water in which they soaked in large pot. If necessary, add sufficient water to cover beans completely. Add remaining ingredients (except rice and green onion). Cover and cook over low heat until beans are tender—about 1 to 1½ hours.

Purée about one-third of the beans to a smooth, fairly thick paste in an electric blender with some of the water in which they cooked. Drain remaining beans of all but about 2 tablespoons of water, add the rice, bean purée, and green onion. Fork-stir, over medium heat, until mixture is thoroughly heated.

[6 *to* 8 *servings as a main course;* 8 *to* 12 *servings as a side dish.*]

NOTE: If you do not have a blender, mash beans and stir in enough bean water to make a thick purée.

CHINESE FRIED RICE

¼ cup peanut oil
3 cups cold boiled rice
¾ to 1 cup shredded leftover
    lean pork, veal, or beef; or
    boiled or roasted chicken,
    ham, or lobster; or diced
    boiled shrimp or flaked crab-
    meat; or 2 to 4 slices of
    crumbled crisp-cooked bacon

3 tablespoons soy sauce
Salt ⎤
Freshly ground ⎬ to taste
    black pepper ⎦
2 eggs, lightly beaten
2 to 3 scallions, chopped

Heat the oil in a heavy skillet. Add the rice and fork-stir over moderate heat until grains are thoroughly coated with oil. Add the shredded meat, chicken, or seafood and continue to cook, stirring, for 3 to 4 minutes. Stir in the soy sauce and season to taste with salt and pepper. Turn heat to high and add the eggs all at once. Stir rapidly until eggs are firm and well blended with rice and meat. Remove from heat and stir in scallions.
[4 servings.]

CURRIED RICE WITH CHICKEN OR SEAFOOD

3 tablespoons butter
1 medium onion
1 tablespoon flour
2 tablespoons curry powder
2 cups chicken stock, canned
    or homemade (see page 203)
1 cup light cream

Salt ⎤
Pepper ⎦ to taste
2 cups cooked rice
1 cup diced cooked chicken,
    lobster, shrimp, or flaked
    crabmeat
¼ cup diced pimiento

Melt the butter in a large skillet. Add the onion and sauté until limp but not browned. Blend in the flour and curry powder. Stir until smooth. Gradually add the stock and cream, blend, and stir over low heat until sauce thickens. Season to taste with salt and pepper.

Add the rice and chicken or seafood and pimiento. Fork-stir to blend. Turn heat to low and cook without stirring for a final 2 to 3 minutes.
[6 *servings.*]

SECOND GENERATION CHINESE FRIED RICE

1 *medium onion, chopped*
½ *small green pepper, chopped*
2 *to 3 ribs celery*
1 *tablespoon vegetable oil*
1 *tablespoon butter*

2 *cups cold boiled rice*
1 *tablespoon soy sauce*
Freshly ground
  black pepper } *to taste*
Salt

In large heavy skillet, sauté onion, green pepper, and celery in combined oil and butter until crisp-tender. Add rice, stir to blend, and cook, stirring with fork, until rice is heated. Blend in soy sauce and season to taste with pepper and salt.
[4 *servings.*]

QUICK JAMBALAYA

2 *thick slices smoked bacon, diced*
1 *medium onion, chopped*
½ *small green pepper, chopped, free of all seeds and fiber*
1 *small clove garlic, minced*
3 *cups cold boiled rice*
1 *cup (canned) tomatoes and juice*

1 *teaspoon tomato paste*
½ *to 1 cup diced boiled or baked ham or chicken or combination of both*
8 *to 12 boiled shrimp (optional)*
Salt
Freshly ground } *to taste*
  black pepper

Place bacon in a deep heavy skillet. Cook over low heat until crisp, remove with slotted spoon. Drain on absorbent paper. Set aside. Remove all but about 1 tablespoon of the bacon fat from the skillet. Add onion, green pepper, and garlic. Cook, stirring frequently, until vegetables are limp. Add remaining ingredients and reserved bacon. Fork-stir until well

blended. Cover skillet. Turn heat to low and let mixture cook until thoroughly heated.
[6 *servings.*]

BAKED RICE

3 *cups cold boiled rice*
¾ *cup grated sharp cheddar cheese*
2 *eggs, lightly beaten*
1 *small onion, finely chopped*
1 *small green pepper, finely chopped, free of all seeds and fiber*

Salt ⎱ *to taste*
Pepper ⎰
¼ *to* ½ *cup sliced pimiento, stuffed olives, slivered ripe olives, or diced pimiento (optional)*

Combine all ingredients, mix well. Place in a buttered casserole and bake at 350° for 25 to 30 minutes. Cover casserole for last 5 to 10 minutes of baking if mixture seems too dry.
[4 *to* 6 *servings.*]

TEXAS RICE HASH

1 *large onion, chopped*
1 *small green pepper, seeded and chopped*
1½ *tablespoons vegetable oil*
1 *tablespoon butter*
1 *lb. ground beef*
2 *cups (canned) tomatoes with juice*

1 *cup cooked rice*
1 *teaspoon chili sauce*
1 *teaspoon salt*
½ *teaspoon pepper*
Crumbled or grated Monterey Jack cheese

Sauté onion and green pepper in heavy skillet in the combined oil and butter until crisp-tender. Add ground beef and cook, stirring, until it is no longer pink. Stir in tomatoes, add rice and seasonings. Allow to simmer gently for 8 to 10 minutes. Sprinkle cheese over surface. Cover skillet and cook until cheese has melted.
[4 *to* 6 *servings.*]

OLD-FASHIONED RICE PUDDING

4 *eggs, lightly beaten*
2 *cups milk*
¾ *cup sugar*
⅛ *teaspoon salt*
¼ *teaspoon cinnamon*

¼ *teaspoon nutmeg*
½ *teaspoon vanilla*
2 *cups cold boiled rice*
½ *cup raisins*

Combine all ingredients, in order listed, in large mixing bowl and blend well. Transfer to a buttered deep baking dish or casserole. Bake at 300° until firm—about 30 minutes. Serve warm or cold with ice cream or sweetened whipped cream.

[6 *servings.*]

ROYAL RICE PUDDING
WITH PEACH SAUCE GRAND MARNIER

3 *cups cold boiled rice*
¾ *cup sugar*
¼ *cup Grand Marnier*
1 *cup whipping cream*

1 *package gelatin*
2 *tablespoons cold water*
Peach sauce Grand Marnier
   (*see page* 122)

Mix the rice with sugar and Grand Marnier. Whip cream until stiff, fold into rice. Sprinkle gelatin over cold water in saucepan, stir over low heat until dissolved, add to rice-cream mixture. Blend well and pour into a chilled mold. Refrigerate until firm. Unmold. Serve with peach sauce Grand Marnier.

[6 *servings.*]

PEACH SAUCE GRAND MARNIER

¼ *cup currant jelly*   ¼ *cup Grand Marnier*
¼ *cup water*
1 *package frozen peaches,*
  crushed

Heat jelly with water in saucepan over low heat. Remove from heat and cool. Add peaches and Grand Marnier. Refrigerate until ready to use.

Pasta and Beans

Pasta

PASTA MUST ONLY BE SERVED when freshly cooked, says the would-be gourmet—but he eats his own words every time he rhapsodizes over the wonderful fruit kugel he "discovered" in Vienna, over macaroni salad as served in New Orleans, or over any one of the numerous other epicurean dishes made from cooked pasta that have long been known to generations of thrifty good cooks.

While it certainly is true that boiled pasta—from spaghetti to linguini—cannot be reheated successfully in its original form, noodles, macaroni, and such can be combined with other ingredients and recooked. The results can be very good—often great.

TO STORE: Refrigerate well-drained pasta lightly coated with oil in covered dish; use within two days. Or (preferred method), as soon as possible after first serving prepare but do not cook recipe with leftover pasta. Place in baking dish and seal dish with foil. Refrigerate; cook within two days. Or, freeze and store in freezer; cook within six weeks.

EASY BAKED MACARONI

3 cups cooked macaroni
¾ cup chopped or sliced
   mushrooms
3 tablespoons butter
¾ cup creamy cottage cheese
6 tablespoons grated Parmesan
   cheese

1 cup cream
¼ teaspoon salt
¼ teaspoon freshly ground
   black pepper
2 tablespoons melted butter
Paprika

Place one-third of the macaroni in a well-buttered baking dish. Sprinkle with one-third of the mushrooms. Cover with slivers of butter, top with one-third of the cottage cheese, and sprinkle 2 tablespoons of the grated Parmesan cheese over the surface.

Combine cream, salt, and pepper. Add about one-third of this mixture to the dish. Repeat layers twice again. Pour melted butter over surface and sprinkle with paprika. Bake in a preheated 350° oven for 25 to 30 minutes.
[4 *servings.*]

KUGEL

3 *cups cooked broad noodles*   6 *eggs, well beaten*
½ *cup chicken fat (substitute*   Salt
   butter if desired)   *Freshly ground black pepper*

Combine noodles, chicken fat, and eggs. Season with salt and pepper. Place in well-buttered deep baking dish. Bake in preheated 400° oven until surface is lightly brown and kugel is firm.
[6 *servings.*]

PAN-FRIED NOODLES

2 *cups cooked flat noodles*   ½ *teaspoon salt*
4 *eggs*   ½ *cup crumbled soft cheddar*
2 *tablespoons minced chives*   *cheese*
3 *tablespoons cream*   8 *tablespoons butter*

Plunge noodles into boiling salted water. Allow water to return to full boil. Remove noodles from heat immediately and drain.

Beat the eggs with the chives, cream, and salt. Combine with the noodles and crumbled cheese.

Heat 6 tablespoons of the butter in a heavy skillet. Add the noodle mixture and cook without stirring until underside is lightly browned. Place a large flat plate over the skillet, invert, and turn the noodles out in one piece. Add the remaining butter to the skillet, let it melt, then slide the noodles, moist side down, back into the skillet. Cook until second side is browned. Turn out, cut into pie-shaped wedges, and serve. [4 *to* 6 *servings.*]

NOODLE PIE

*Unbaked pastry for 2-crust pie
  (see page 220)*
½ cup milk
2 cups cooked flat noodles
*1 cup minced baked or boiled
  ham*

*1 tablespoon butter, cut into
  thin slivers*
3 tablespoons sour cream
3 tablespoons minced onion
Freshly ground black pepper
Salt, if needed

Line a 9-inch pie pan with pastry. Refrigerate until well chilled. Chill pastry for top crust.

Heat milk (do not allow to boil) and pour over noodles in large bowl. Let noodles soak for 2 to 3 minutes, then place in colander and drain off milk.

Line chilled dough in pan with one-third of the drained noodles. Cover with one-third of the ham. Dot with 1 tea-spoon of the butter slivers, add 1 tablespoon of sour cream, 1 tablespoon minced onion, and a generous sprinkling of pepper. Add salt to taste (quantity depends on saltiness of ham). Repeat layers twice again. Cover with pastry dough, seal edges. Prick surface several times with fork. Place in a preheated 400° oven and bake for 10 minutes; reduce heat to 325° and bake for 20 to 25 minutes, or until crust is a light golden brown. Serve hot or cold. Cut in thin wedges as an appetizer or serve larger portions as an entree. [8 *servings as an appetizer; 4 servings as an entree.*]

MACARONI SALAD NEW ORLEANS

3 *cups cold cooked elbow macaroni*
1 *cup thinly sliced celery*
½ *cup finely minced green pepper*
¼ *cup finely minced green onion*
½ *cup chopped sweet pickles*
¾ *cup mayonnaise*
1 *teaspoon lemon juice*
Salt
Freshly ground black pepper } *to taste*
Lettuce

Combine all ingredients (except lettuce) and blend well. Refrigerate in nonmetal bowl covered with foil or plastic wrap for 3 hours or longer to allow flavors to mellow. Serve from lettuce-lined bowl.
[6 *to* 8 *servings.*]

FRUIT KUGEL

3 *eggs, separated*
⅓ *cup brown sugar*
¼ *teaspoon cinnamon*
⅛ *teaspoon nutmeg*
3 *cups cooked broad noodles*
½ *cup seedless white raisins*
1 *tart apple, cored, peeled, and chopped*
½ *cup chopped walnuts*
4 *tablespoons melted butter or chicken fat*

Beat the egg yolks with the sugar until fluffy. Add the cinnamon and nutmeg, blend, and add the noodles, raisins, apple, walnuts, and melted butter. Beat the egg whites until stiff and fold into the noodle mixture. Transfer to a well-buttered deep baking dish. Bake in a preheated 375° oven for 45 to 50 minutes.

Serve plain or with fruit sauce (see page 208).
[6 *servings.*]

Baked Beans

NOTHING SUITS SO WELL on a cold winter's night as homemade baked beans—and they will be good the next night, too (but really more welcome a week or two later). It's wonderful to know that they freeze well and will keep in the freezer for three or four months.

TO STORE: Place in airtight container. Refrigerate up to one week. Or, pack meal-size portions in airtight container and freeze; store in freezer up to four months.

BITS AND PIECES

Mash beans and combine with equal parts chili sauce or piccalilli. Spread on melba toast rounds. Serve as appetizer.

Tear out soft centers from hamburger buns. Fill with baked beans. Cover beans with bacon strips. Broil until bacon is crisp.

Mash beans into hot mashed potatoes, sprinkle with mild grated cheese. Run under a hot broiler just before serving.

Scoop out center of boiled onions and fill with baked beans. Dot with butter and dust with bread crumbs. Bake in a medium oven until piping hot.

Mash beans, bind with beaten egg (1 egg to each 2 cups of beans). Form into small flat cakes. Fry in butter, turning once, until crisp and lightly browned.

BAKED BEAN SANDWICH

1 *cup baked beans, with sauce*
½ *cup chopped mixed pickles*
¼ *cup chopped onion*
Mayonnaise, enough to bind bean mixture, or, as substitute, chili sauce

Boston brown bread, or, as substitute, light rye bread
Butter

Mash beans. Combine with pickles and onion, add sufficient mayonnaise to form a smooth spread.

Spread bread lightly with butter, heavily with bean mixture. Makes enough spread for 4 sandwiches.

BAKED BEAN CROQUETTES

2 *cups baked beans*
1 *tablespoon chili sauce, more if beans are dry*
1 *medium onion, minced*

1 *egg, lightly beaten*
1 *cup peanuts, ground or chopped very fine*
Vegetable oil for deep frying

Mash beans with chili sauce until smooth. Add onion, blend, and form mixture into small balls.

Dip balls in beaten egg. Roll in peanuts. Refrigerate for 2 hours or longer.

Fry balls in very hot deep fat (375°) until lightly browned. Drain on paper toweling.
[4 *to* 6 *servings.*]

Boiled Kidney Beans

BITS AND PIECES

Add leftover boiled kidney beans to beef or lamb stews during last few minutes of cooking. Add to vegetable or other soups and to green or vegetable salads. Or marinate in garlicky French dressing and drain just before serving as part of an Italian antipasto or as an appetizer with smoked salmon.

To each cup cold beans, add ½ cup chopped celery, ¼ cup each chopped onion and green pepper. Add sufficient mayonnaise to bind, plus salt and pepper to taste, and serve as a salad.

BEANS AND RICE JAMAICAN STYLE

2 tablespoons butter
1 cup boiled kidney beans
1 cup cooked long-grain rice
¼ cup shredded coconut

Salt
Pepper } to taste
Pinch of thyme

Melt butter in a large heavy skillet. Add the kidney beans, rice, and coconut. Cook, stirring gently with fork, until well heated. Season with salt and pepper and a pinch of thyme. [4 to 6 servings.]

KIDNEY BEAN AND ONION SALAD

2 large sweet red onions
2 cups cold cooked kidney
   beans
⅓ cup olive oil
2 tablespoons red wine vinegar

Salt
Freshly ground } to taste
   black pepper
Lettuce
Anchovy fillets

Peel and cut onions into paper-thin slices. Break slices into rings and place in nonmetal bowl. Cover with ice water and let stand for 30 minutes. Drain, pat dry, and combine with beans. Add oil and vinegar, blend, and add salt and pepper to taste. Serve on crisp lettuce leaves. Garnish each serving with anchovy fillets.

[6 *servings.*]

MEXICAN REFRIED BEANS

2 *thick slices of bacon*
2 *cups cooked kidney or other red or pink beans*
½ *cup liquid from cooked beans (substitute chicken stock if desired)*

Salt
Pepper } *to taste*

Cook the bacon in a large skillet over very low heat until all fat has been rendered and bacon is crisp.

Remove bacon, drain on paper toweling, crumble, and set aside.

Add beans to skillet, about ¼ cup at a time, mashing them into the bacon drippings. Stir in about 2 tablespoons of the bean liquid. If there is not sufficient bean liquid substitute chicken stock or water. Repeat until all beans and liquid have been used. Continue mashing and stirring over low heat until beans have the consistency of thick mashed potatoes.

Season with salt and pepper. Add the crumbled bacon if desired or reserve it for another dish.

[6 *servings.*]

VARIATIONS

Substitute tomato paste for bean liquid. Stir in 1 tablespoon chili powder.

Or, when all beans have been mashed, stir in ¼ to ½ cup mild grated cheese.

Or, after bacon has been removed, add 1 small chopped

onion to bacon drippings, stir over low heat until onion is
limp but not brown, then proceed with recipe.

FRIJOLAS
(Red Beans in Sauce)

4 oz. salt pork, cubed	2 cups boiled kidney beans
1 large red onion, chopped	½ teaspoon chili powder
1 small green pepper, chopped	Salt
1 8-oz. can tomato sauce	Pepper } to taste
½ cup water	Freshly cooked white rice

Cook salt pork in large heavy skillet over very low heat
until crisp. Pour off all but about 2 tablespoons fat from skillet.
Add onion and green pepper and cook, stirring often, until
vegetables are limp. Add remaining ingredients (except rice)
and cook over low heat for 15 to 20 minutes. Serve over just-
cooked hot white rice.
[4 to 6 servings.]

Boiled Beans

NAVY and White Beans, Dried Lima Beans, and Black-eyed Peas.

BITS AND PIECES

Use as suggested for kidney beans.

Or, reheat in spicy tomato sauce, cream sauce with cheese, chicken or beef stock, or brown sauce.

Cover cold drained beans with French dressing. Add a clove of garlic, let marinate for 30 minutes or longer, then drain. Mix with chopped crisp radishes and chopped unpeeled cucumber. Add a small amount of mayonnaise, toss, and serve on crisp leaves of spinach or romaine.

PICKLED BEANS

2 *cups cooked beans, drained*	1 *small white onion, chopped*
½ *cup salad oil*	½ *teaspoon salt*
½ *cup chopped mixed sweet pickles with juice*	⅛ *teaspoon freshly ground black pepper*
1 *clove garlic, split*	1 *tablespoon tarragon vinegar*

Place beans in nonmetal bowl. Add remaining ingredients. Toss lightly to blend. Cover and refrigerate for 12 hours or longer. Drain and serve as salad or as part of an antipasto platter.
[4 *servings.*]

BEAN LOAF

2 *cups cooked dried beans*   1 *tablespoon butter*
2 *eggs, well beaten*   Salt ⎤
2 *tablespoons chili sauce*   Pepper ⎰ *to taste*
1 *cup bread crumbs*   3 *tablespoons apricot jam*
1 *small onion, chopped*   1 *tablespoon water*

Mash beans slightly. Add eggs, chili sauce, and bread crumbs.

Sauté onion in butter until limp but not brown. Add to bean mixture. Blend well and season to taste with salt and pepper. Shape into a loaf. Place in shallow baking pan and bake in preheated 350° oven for 20 minutes.

Heat jam and water in small saucepan over low heat until the jam melts. Spoon over surface of bean loaf. Bake for a final 5 to 10 minutes, or until loaf is glazed.

Serve with broiled bacon or slices of baked ham.

[6 *servings.*]

Fruit

Apples—Baked

PEEL, CHOP, and add to fruit salads for a change in taste.

Dice and mix with corn flakes or other dry cereal before adding sugar and milk.

Peel, mash, and blend with a small amount of cognac, other brandy, or apple cider. Serve over vanilla ice cream.

Blend into sweetened whipped cream. Use as topping for plain cakes or pudding.

RIGHT SIDE UP UPSIDE DOWN APPLE CAKE

¼ cup apple cider
1 9-inch cake layer (you may buy it or bake it)

2 baked apples
2 to 4 tablespoons butter

Pour the cider over the cake layer. Peel and mash the baked apples and spread over the surface of the cake. Sprinkle with slivers of butter. Place about 4 inches under broiler flame and broil until surface is lightly browned and crusty. Serve warm. [6 to 8 servings.]

APPLESAUCE

Fold ⅓ to ¾ cup cold applesauce into a pint of soft vanilla ice cream. Add ¼ cup bourbon or blended whiskey. Blend quickly but well. Pour into ice cube tray or mold. Freeze until firm. Makes a lovely "what's in it?" dessert.

Mix applesauce with creamy cottage cheese and chopped nuts (½ cup applesauce to 1 cup cottage cheese and ¼ cup walnuts or pecans). Use ice cream scoop to form mixture into 4 balls. Place each in the center of an individual salad bowl lined with crisp lettuce. Surround with fresh fruit, garnish with mayonnaise.

Mash applesauce with cream cheese and cream (½ cup applesauce, 1 3-oz. package cream cheese, 2 or 3 tablespoons cream). Spread on Boston brown bread.

APRICOT SAUCE

1 *cup stewed* (*unsweetened*)
  apricots
½ *cup water or liquid from*
  stewed apricots

¾ *cup sugar*
1 *teaspoon lemon juice*
2 *tablespoons kirsch*

Purée apricots with water in electric blender, or press apricots through a sieve and combine with water. Place in saucepan. Add sugar and cook, stirring, over low heat until sauce is thick and smooth. Remove from heat, add lemon juice and kirsch. Serve hot or refrigerate. Serve chilled or reheat. Makes about 1½ cups sauce.

NOTE: Use sweetened apricots if desired. Adjust quantity of sugar to taste. Also, stewed peaches may be substituted for apricots, peach brandy for kirsch.

Bananas—Overripe

TO STORE: *Refrigerate them. Contrary to all you have been told, though the skins will turn unattractively dark, refrigeration will in no way affect the fruit. It will, however, inhibit further ripening. Use within two or three days.*

Broil overripe bananas and cover with meringue. Refrigerate. Serve as a glamour dessert within two or three days.

HOW TO: *Peel and slice bananas lengthwise. Place in shallow baking dish. Sprinkle with lemon juice and sugar. Dot with slivers of butter. Bake bananas in a 350° oven until cooked but still firm —about 20 minutes. Beat egg white until stiff, fold in sugar (2 tablespoons sugar to each egg white). Spread meringue over bananas, covering them completely. Place in preheated 450° oven until meringue is lightly browned.*

Mash overripe bananas with sugar and lemon juice (about ½ teaspoon lemon juice and 1 tablespoon sugar for each banana). Fold into sweetened whipped cream (1 cup cream for each 4 or 5 bananas). Pack in mold, wrap mold completely in foil. Store in freezer up to six weeks.

Or, pack mixture in cookie-crumb crust. Wrap and freeze in the same way.

Berries—Fresh

BLACKBERRIES, Raspberries, Boysenberries, and Strawberries.

If you are fortunate enough to have too many ripe berries on hand, make fresh berry sauce and freeze it to use any time.

Wash, drain, and press berries through a sieve. Add ½ cup sugar to each 2 cups of sieved berries. Stir until sugar has dissolved. Pack in airtight containers, leaving ½ inch of space at top to allow for expansion. Freeze; store in freezer for up to six months. Use for sauces or frozen desserts.

Canned Fruit

BITS AND PIECES

Suggestions for those leftover 2 or more peach, pear, or apricot halves:

Combine equal parts mayonnaise and unsweetened whipped cream. Spread on peach halves. Broil until surface of topping is flecked with brown. Serve with baked ham.

Spread pear halves with mint jelly. Place on foil or in shallow pan. Bake in 350° oven only until pears are thoroughly heated. Serve with lamb.

Spread sour cream on apricot halves. Place a dot of currant jelly in the center. Bake in 350° oven only until apricots are thoroughly heated. Serve with broiled fish.

Heat peach halves in butter, sprinkle with sugar. Serve with roast pork.

Brush peach halves with melted butter. Place on foil or in shallow pan, cut side down. Sprinkle liberally with sugar. Place under broiler heat until "glazed." Serve with chicken à la king.

Dice leftover canned fruit, add to warm zabaglione or any custard sauce. Serve over ice cream or plain cake.

Dice and mix any canned fruit with an equal amount of fresh sliced bananas. Heat in a chafing dish with equal parts canned fruit juice and butter. Sprinkle liberally with sugar. Pour warm cognac, other brandy, or kirsch over surface. Tilt pan toward flame so that liqueur ignites. Flame mixture for a few seconds, then serve flaming over vanilla ice cream.

PEARS HÉLÈNE

For each serving:

1 *scoop vanilla ice cream*　　2 *to* 3 *tablespoons chocolate*
1 *pear half*　　　　　　　　　　*sauce, heated*
　　　　　　　　　　　　　　　　Whipped cream

Place ice cream in individual dessert bowl. Cover with pear half. Spoon hot sauce over surface. Garnish with whipped cream.

QUICK PEACH MELBA

For each serving:

2 *to* 3 *tablespoons Melba*　　1 *scoop vanilla ice cream*
　sauce (*commercially*　　　　1 *peach half*
　bottled)　　　　　　　　　　　*Whipped cream*

Spoon a little Melba sauce into the bottom of a parfait glass. Add ice cream. Cover with peach, top with Melba sauce. Garnish with whipped cream.

Citrus Fruit Rind

ORANGE AND LEMON.

Grate zest (orange or yellow part) from leftover orange or lemon rind. Pack in small plastic bag or in foil and place in small container with airtight cover. Use frozen or thawed as garnish or as seasoning in sauces, custards, cakes, or what-will-you.

CANDIED ORANGE SHELLS

After squeezing oranges, store rinds in plastic bag in refrigerator. When ready to use them, place rinds in a large saucepan and cover with water. Bring to boil, lower heat, and simmer until tender. Drain and combine with sugar and cold water (1 cup sugar, 1 cup water for each 6 orange shells). Place over low heat and simmer for 30 minutes. Cool in syrup. Drain. Refrigerate in plastic bag until ready to use.

Fill with cranberry sauce or mint or currant jelly; use as garnish for baked ham or roasted duck. Or, fill with ice cream and serve as dessert; or, chop and sprinkle over custard, ice cream, or plain cake.

LEMON OR ORANGE BEIGNETS

1 *cup water*
¼ *lb. sweet butter*
2 *teaspoons grated orange or lemon rind*
1 *cup sifted all-purpose flour*
2 *tablespoons sugar*

5 *eggs*
2 *tablespoons curaçao*
Oil or shortening for deep frying
Confectioners' sugar

Combine water, butter, and grated rind in large saucepan. Place over heat until butter has melted and water is boiling.

Remove from heat and add flour all at once. Stir vigorously until mixture leaves the sides of the pan. Beat in the sugar with one egg. Add the remaining eggs, one at a time, beating after each addition. Add the curaçao and continue to beat to a smooth dough.

Fill a deep heavy saucepan with oil or melted shortening to within 2 inches of rim. Heat to 380° on deep fat thermometer (or until small cubes of white bread will brown in 30 seconds). Drop dough by spoonfuls (a few at a time) into the hot fat. Fry to a deep golden brown. Remove with slotted spoon, drain on paper toweling, then roll in confectioners' sugar. Serve warm with fruit sauce (see page 208) or serve when cool as a "go with" for coffee or tea.

[*Makes about* 36 *beignets.*]

Cranberries—Ripe, More Than You Care to Cook

TO STORE: Place on flat tray in freezer until very firm. Scoop into plastic bags and store in freezer up to six months.

EASY CRANBERRY-ORANGE RELISH

1 *orange*
½ *cup sugar*

¼ *cup frozen raw cranberries*
¼ *cup candied ginger*

Quarter orange and remove seeds. Remove and discard rind from three of the sections. Put orange sections with remaining rind and sugar in electric blender. Blend at low speed to a purée, add cranberries and candied ginger. Blend until cranberries are chopped. Chill well before serving.
[*Makes about 1 cup relish.*]

Dates

TO STORE: The best way to keep them fresh is to freeze them. Remove pits, pack in plastic bags, press out all air, and seal bags. Great to eat right from the freezer.

BITS AND PIECES

Snip with kitchen shears into salads. Snip and add to cream sauce for chicken, seafood, or vegetables. Combine with chopped crisp apples and chopped walnuts, bind with mayonnaise. Serve on crisp lettuce leaves.

Wrap whole pitted dates in strips of bacon. Broil until bacon is crisp. Serve as hot hors d'oeuvre.

Stuff pitted dates with cream cheese ("creamed" with a little milk and mixed with chopped chives).

Or, stuff pitted dates with chopped salted peanuts, walnut halves, pecan halves, candied ginger, or well-drained crushed pineapple mixed with softened cream cheese.

LOUISIANA DATE LOAF CANDY

½ *cup milk*　　　　　　　1½ *cups sugar*
1 *cup pitted dates*　　　　2 *cups chopped pecans*

Place milk, dates, and sugar in electric blender, blend until smooth. Transfer to saucepan. Cook, stirring, until mixture leaves the sides of the pan. Turn out onto a large napkin that has been wrung out in cold water. Form into a "log," roll log in chopped pecans, then wrap in a damp napkin. Chill until firm. Cut into thin slices and serve.

Fruit Jam

THAT LITTLE bit left in the bottom of the jar.

Store in airtight jar in dry place. If jam has become granular, place the jar in a pan of warm water until sugar crystals have disappeared (15 to 30 minutes).

Add to jar with that last bit of jam an equal amount of cognac, other brandy, or kirsch. Cover jar and shake vigorously. Use as is, or heat. Serve as sauce over ice cream, custard, or cake.

Grapes—Those Last Few

ADD TO BOTH fruit salad or green salad of course, but also to salads of chicken or turkey.

Cut grapes in half, remove seeds, and combine with just-cooked, drained Brussels sprouts or chopped broccoli, or add to cream sauce for fish.

Dip grapes in lightly beaten egg white, roll in granulated sugar. Place on cake rack to dry. Use as garnish for fruit platters or for platters of cold roasted chicken or duck, or serve with after-dinner coffee instead of a more fattening dessert.

Place small clusters of white grapes with stem in jar. Cover with brandy or blended whiskey. Cover jar and refrigerate for 24 hours or longer. Serve with cocktails.

SAUCE VÉRONIQUE

Trimmings: head and bones	1 *slice of onion*
from 2 lbs. of sole (your fish-	¼ *teaspoon salt*
man will give them to you)	⅛ *teaspoon pepper*
½ *cup dry white wine*	2 *tablespoons butter*
¾ *cup water*	2 *tablespoons flour*
1 *tablespoon lemon juice*	1 *cup light cream*
1 *sprig parsley*	¾ *cup seedless white grapes*

Place trimmings (head and bones from fish), wine, water, lemon juice, parsley, onion, salt, and pepper in saucepan. Simmer gently over low heat for 30 minutes. Strain.

Melt butter in a second saucepan. Stir in flour. When flour is blended in, slowly add the fish stock, stirring it into the flour-butter mixture as it is added. Stir until smooth, then add cream, and continue stirring until mixture becomes a smooth thick sauce. Correct seasoning with salt. Add grapes, blend, and serve over baked or poached sole or other similar fish. [*Makes enough sauce for 4 servings of fish.*]

Raisins

DRIED OUT: cover with boiling water and allow to stand until "plumped up" (2 or 3 minutes). Drain and use.

Those last few raisins:
Add to fruit salads, sprinkle over green salad. Stir into hot cooked cereal, add to custards, cookie and muffin batter, or to tea biscuit dough. Add to sweet-and-sour sauce or curry sauce. Blend with grated orange rind into hot, just-cooked white or brown rice or into wild rice.

CUMBERLAND SAUCE WITH RAISINS

½ cup currant jelly
¼ cup lemon juice
½ cup orange juice
½ teaspoon grated lemon or orange rind
Raisins, about ¼ cup

Combine all ingredients but raisins. Beat with wire whisk until blended. Stir in raisins. Chill. Serve with cold meats. Especially good with cold roast pork, lamb, or tongue.
[*Makes about 1 cup sauce.*]

SWEET-AND-SOUR SAUCE

For fried or baked chicken, boiled shrimp or other fish:

1 cup chicken stock, canned or homemade (see page 203)
½ cup bamboo shoots, sliced
1 clove garlic, minced
1 tablespoon dry sherry
1 tablespoon brown sugar
1 tablespoon soy sauce
1 tablespoon cornstarch
1 tablespoon water
¼ to ½ cup raisins

Combine stock, bamboo shoots, and garlic in saucepan. Bring to boil, lower heat, and stir in sherry, brown sugar, and soy sauce. Simmer gently for 5 minutes. Blend cornstarch and water. Add to saucepan. Cook, stirring, until sauce thickens. Add raisins.

Serve hot.

[*Makes enough sauce for 4 servings.*]

Stewed Fruit

DRIED APRICOTS, apples, prunes, peaches, pears, or mixed dried fruit.

BITS AND PIECES

Snip with kitchen shears into small pieces, add to just-cooked hot lima beans, green beans, Brussels sprouts, chopped broccoli or spinach. Add a pat of butter, a squeeze of lemon, and a sprinkling of sugar. Stir over low heat until butter has melted.

Cover stewed fruit with port wine. Cover and refrigerate for 24 hours or longer. Serve in dessert bowls with a scoop of vanilla ice cream.

Make a fruit shake—2 or 3 stewed apricots, pears, prunes, or peaches, 2 tablespoons frozen orange juice, 2 cups milk. Whirl in electric blender until smooth.

Add drained stewed fruit to a fresh fruit salad or to a salad of mixed greens.

Purée stewed fruit in blender. Mix with equal amount of cream cheese. Use as spread for date-nut bread.

Purée stewed fruit in blender. To each ½ cup puréed fruit, add 1 tablespoon lemon juice, ½ cup honey. Use as glaze for baked ham or ham loaf.

Purée stewed fruit in blender. Mix with boiled frosting. Use as filling for layer cakes.

Dice stewed fruit and blend with homemade mayonnaise. Use as dressing for fruit salad, or serve with cold roasted chicken.

Dice stewed fruit and combine with diced ripe avocado. Sprinkle with lemon juice. Bind with mayonnaise or French dressing, blended with mashed ripe avocado. Serve on crisp leaves of romaine.

FRUIT BAKED ALASKAS

6 *squares plain cake*
6 *tablespoons* (*puréed in a*
   blender) *stewed fruit*

6 *small scoops vanilla ice*
   cream
Meringue—see below

Scoop out centers from cake squares. Place a tablespoon puréed fruit in each. Add a scoop of ice cream. Place on ovenproof platter. Cover each completely with a thick layer of meringue. Place in a preheated 450° oven until meringue is lightly browned. Serve at once.
[6 *servings.*]

MERINGUE

2 *egg whites*   6 *tablespoons sugar*

Beat egg whites until they will stand in peaks. Beat in sugar, a teaspoon at a time. Use at once.

LEFTOVER JUICE FROM CANNED FRUIT

Freeze in ice cube trays. When juice is frozen, transfer to plastic bags and store in freezer. Use for iced tea or fruit punch, or thaw and use for fruit sauce.

Dairy Products

Dairy Products

SUCH STAPLES as cream, cheese, and eggs are rarely thought of as "leftovers"; yet very often they are just that.

What to do with the whipped cream from last night's party and how to make use of those extra egg yolks are problems that are often dismissed—until it's too late.

If you would cut down on your food bills, learn to shop your refrigerator before you grocery shop. Plan menus that make good use of these very perishable foods *before* they are fit only to be thrown out.

Cream

TO STORE: Leftover cream can be frozen. Place in freezer container, leave space at top for expansion, wrap container in foil, and freeze; use within six weeks. Thaw heavy cream in refrigerator before whipping. Use light cream directly from freezer for cooking.

WHIPPED CREAM

Pack leftover whipped cream—sweetened or unsweetened—in airtight container. Store in freezer. Thaw unsweetened cream in refrigerator before using. Use sweetened whipped cream as dessert topping; thawing is not necessary.

WHIPPED CREAM BALLS

Use a pastry bag or a spoon to shape sweetened whipped cream into neat mounds on a cookie sheet. Freeze until firm, then pack in freezer container. Mounds will not stick together. Use frozen as needed and serve as topping for pies, custards, or cakes.

Fold into whipped cream before shaping into mounds: chopped blanched almonds, grated orange rind, puréed fresh or stewed fruit, chopped maraschino cherries. Flavor with: almond extract, vanilla, juice from maraschino cherries, orange juice, cognac, or any other brandy or liqueur.

Unsweetened unflavored whipped cream may be frozen in the same way. Thaw at room temperature for 5 to 10 minutes before using as garnish or topping for hot or cold soup.

FROZEN HORSERADISH WHIPPED CREAM

¼ to ½ cup grated fresh
  horseradish
1 teaspoon sugar
2 tablespoons cognac or other
  good brandy

1 cup leftover unsweetened
  whipped cream

Fold horseradish, sugar, and cognac or other brandy into whipped cream. Pack in ice cube tray, cover tray with foil. Seal by pressing foil against side of tray. Freeze until firm. Let stand at room temperature for 15 to 20 minutes. Stir with fork. Pile into small serving bowl. Serve with cold boiled beef, cold corned beef, boiled or baked ham, lamb or pork. [Makes 1⅓ to 1½ cups.]

That Last Bit of Cheese

GRATE ANY LEFTOVER hard cheese. Pack in small container and freeze. Use frozen. Stir into sauces, sprinkle over soup or au gratin dishes. Toss with pasta, or stir with fork into hot rice.

Frozen grated cheese will stay fresh almost indefinitely. You may keep adding grated cheese to same container. Stir to blend each time you add more cheese.

BLEU OR ROQUEFORT

Freeze it if it is not to be used within a week to ten days. Thaw at room temperature.

CHEESE SPREAD THAT KEEPS

1½ cups grated or shredded leftover cheese (any kind)

2 tablespoons cognac or other good brandy

1 3-oz. package cream cheese

2 tablespoons butter

Combine ingredients and blend well. Beat until smooth. Pack into small crock. Cover and refrigerate for 24 hours or longer. Remove from refrigerator 1 to 2 hours before using.

You can keep adding leftover cheese and cognac to replace amounts used. Mixture improves with age and will last indefinitely.

EASY ECONOMICAL CHEESE DIP

3 *to 4 tablespoons sharp left-*
over cheese, diced or
crumbled
½ *pint creamy cottage cheese*
1 *tablespoon chili sauce*
1 *or 2 tablespoons mayonnaise*

2 *or 3 tablespoons cognac or*
other brandy
Dash Worcestershire sauce
Dash Tabasco sauce
Salt ⎫
Freshly ground ⎬ *to taste*
black pepper ⎭

Combine all ingredients in electric blender, blend until
smooth. Chill before serving. Store in refrigerator up to one
week.

NOTE: You can improvise on this theme: Use sherry instead of cognac
or other brandy, substitute Escoffier Sauce Diable for chili sauce, add
minced chives, sweet mixed pickles, or slivered olives. In other words,
season to taste.

CHEESE STRAWS

Make pie crust dough from a mix, or make your own (see
page 220). Roll out on lightly floured board. Sprinkle half
of dough with leftover grated cheese. Cover with other half
of dough. Roll out and cut into narrow strips, about ¼ x 1
inch. Place on cookie sheet and bake in preheated 375° oven
until lightly browned. Serve warm or reheat later. Or, place
cheese straws not touching on flat tray and freeze. When they
are firm, stack them in layers with wax paper between each.
Wrap layers in foil. Store in freezer. Reheat frozen in preheated 350° oven.

Leftover Egg Whites and Yolks

TO STORE: For leftover egg whites, place in airtight container. Refrigerate; use within one week. Or, freeze; label as to quantity (8 egg whites equal about 1 cup) and store in freezer up to six months. Freeze individual egg whites in small plastic ice cube containers. Store in polyethylene bag in freezer.

For leftover egg yolks, place unbroken in small container. Cover with cold water and cover container with foil, plastic wrap, or airtight lid. Or, place individual yolks in small plastic ice cube container and cover with plastic wrap. Use within three days. To freeze: stir (do not beat) 7 or more eggs lightly with salt or sugar, 1 teaspoon salt or 2 teaspoons sugar to each 6 eggs. Place in airtight container. Label as to sugar or salt and quantity (14 egg yolks equal about 1 cup).

Frozen yolks or whites will defrost at room temperature in about 30 minutes. Use as soon as thawed.

THIS AND THAT

Use leftover whites to clarify aspic, to make angel food cake, white cake, cake filling and frosting, kisses, and meringue.

Use leftover yolks to make custard, cooked salad dressing, noodles, egg nog, gold cakes, frozen mousse. Use to thicken sauces.

Use either leftover yolks *or* whites instead of whole eggs to coat food that is to be breaded and fried; add to each yolk or white 1 tablespoon salad oil, 1 teaspoon water. Blend with wire whisk.

In any recipe that calls for 3 or more whole eggs use one

egg yolk in place of one of the whole eggs. Increase liquid in recipe by 1 teaspoon.

Thicken cream or *any* sauce, soup, or gravy with egg yolks (less flour or other thickening agent may then be used; flavor is improved). Beat yolks lightly, stir in a little of the hot sauce. Add yolk mixture to hot sauce, stirring constantly as it is added.

Lighter than noodles and a change in flavor, add egg whites to clear hot soup, stirring rapidly as they are added. Serve at once.

Substitute egg yolk for whole egg when making mayonnaise (see page 223).

Add 1 or 2 extra yolks to boiled or baked custard—just makes it richer. Especially good in custards made from a mix.

Beat egg whites until stiff, fold into just-made boiled custard. Makes a lighter, fluffier dessert.

Cream ½ cup crumbled soft cheese—cheddar, Roquefort, bleu, etc.—with 2 cups heavy cream. Beat 3 egg whites until stiff, fold into creamed cheese. Place in lightly greased mold and freeze until firm. Unmold and serve with small rounds of cocktail rye or French bread.

Beat egg yolks with melted butter cooled to room temperature (1 tablespoon butter for each egg yolk). Place over simmering water. Stir to a thick smooth sauce. Stir in 1 tablespoon lemon juice. Season with salt, pepper, and Tabasco sauce. Serve over steak, fish, or vegetable.

Cook 1 package of any frozen vegetable according to directions. Drain, add a generous pat of butter. Stir over low heat until butter has melted, then quickly stir in 1 beaten egg yolk. Cook, stirring, until a creamy thick sauce is achieved.

Make homemade or commercial sherbet "gourmet" with:
ITALIAN MERINGUE

½ cup sugar
¼ cup water
Pinch of cream of tartar
1 egg white, stiffly beaten

2 tablespoons any appropriate liqueur—kirsch, Cointreau, chartreuse, cherry or apricot brandy, etc.
Sherbet

Combine sugar, water, and cream of tartar in saucepan. Bring to boil, boil without stirring until syrup reaches 240° on candy thermometer (or until small amount dropped from spoon will form a flexible thread). Remove from heat and pour in slow steady stream into stiffly beaten egg white, beating constantly with rotary beater as syrup is added. Cool and add desired liqueur.

Fold meringue into 1 pint of any flavor (soft but still frozen) sherbet. Transfer to soufflé dish or any fairly deep pan. Cover with foil and freeze until firm.

NOTE: You may use ice cream instead of sherbet.

EASY HOLLANDAISE SAUCE

½ cup butter, room temperature
3 egg yolks, lightly beaten
1 tablespoon lemon juice

Salt
White pepper } to taste
1 tablespoon cream, if needed

Combine half of the butter and all the egg yolks and lemon juice in top of double boiler. Place over barely simmering water and stir until butter has melted. Add remaining butter and beat with a wire whisk to a thick smooth sauce.

Season with salt and pepper. Serve warm or refrigerate and reheat.

If sauce curdles while cooking or reheating, beat in 1 tablespoon cream.

[*Makes about 1 cup sauce.*]

BÉARNAISE SAUCE

1 *cup dry white wine*
1 *tablespoon chopped shallots*
1 *bay leaf, crumbled*
¼ *teaspoon freshly ground*
  black pepper
2 *tablespoons chopped parsley*

2 *tablespoons chopped fresh*
  tarragon
4 *egg yolks*
½ *cup melted butter*
Salt, to taste

Combine wine, shallots, bay leaf, pepper, and 1 tablespoon each of chopped parsley and tarragon in saucepan. Bring to boil, lower heat, and simmer very gently until liquid is reduced by half. Remove from heat and strain. Cool slightly and return liquid to saucepan. Add the egg yolks, beating with a wire whisk as they are added. Return pan to very low heat and slowly add melted butter, stirring constantly. Cook, stirring, until sauce coats the spoon. Add the remaining chopped parsley and tarragon and season with salt. Serve over steak, especially filet mignon, or over fish or vegetable. [*Makes about 2 cups sauce.*]

NOTE: Sauce may be kept warm over hot water or covered and refrigerated. Reheat over barely simmering water.

SPAGHETTI ALLA CARBONATA

4 *slices bacon, diced*
1 *1-lb. package spaghetti*
3 *egg yolks, lightly beaten*

1 *cup Parmesan cheese*
¼ *cup chopped parsley*
Freshly ground black pepper

Cook bacon in heavy skillet over low heat; do not drain. While bacon cooks, cook spaghetti according to package di-

rections. Drain and place in deep serving dish. Add the beaten egg yolks and toss with two forks until egg yolks are well blended with the spaghetti. Pour the hot bacon and bacon fat over surface, add cheese, parsley, and black pepper. Toss again until all ingredients are blended. Serve at once.
[4 *servings*.]

PLAIN CUSTARD SAUCE

6 *egg yolks*   ¼ *cup sugar*
2 *cups milk, scalded, hot*   ¼ *teaspoon vanilla*

Beat egg yolks in top half of double boiler. Add hot milk and sugar. Cook, stirring, over hot but not boiling water until mixture coats the spoon. Remove from heat and add vanilla. Serve hot or cold.
[4 *servings*.]

VARIATIONS

GRAND MARNIER SAUCE

Substitute 3 tablespoons Grand Marnier for vanilla.

SHERRY SAUCE

Substitute 3 tablespoons sherry for vanilla.

RUM SAUCE

Substitute 3 tablespoons rum—light or dark—for vanilla. Cool sauce and fold in ½ cup whipped cream.

CURAÇAO SAUCE

Substitute 3 tablespoons curaçao for vanilla. Add 1 teaspoon grated orange rind.

MOCHA SAUCE

Blend 3 tablespoons strong cold coffee with milk before scalding. Proceed as in making plain custard sauce. Before removing sauce from heat, add 2 tablespoons grated semi-sweet chocolate to hot sauce and stir until melted.

CLASSIC ZABAGLIONE

6 *egg yolks*
1 *cup sugar*
¼ *teaspoon grated orange or*
   lemon rind

1 *cup Marsala, or, as substi-*
   tute, any sweet white wine

Beat egg yolks and sugar with wire whisk in top half of double boiler until very pale in color. Add orange or lemon rind and wine. Beat until blended. Place over simmering water and continue to beat until mixture is very thick and smooth. Spoon into small dessert cups or bowl, and serve warm.
[4 *to* 6 *servings.*]

NOTE: As Zabaglione is very rich, small portions are in order.

Warm Zabaglione may also be served as a sauce over chilled poached fresh fruit or over stewed or canned fruit. Or, serve over plain cake or in parfait glasses lined with lady-fingers that have been soaked in a bit of the same wine used in the Zabaglione. For another variation, spoon Zabaglione into dessert plates and place a scoop of vanilla ice cream in the center. Or, serve over bread or rice pudding.

Leftover Hard-cooked Eggs

YOU CAN STUFF HARD-COOKED EGGS, of course, for use as appetizers or in lunch boxes, for picnics and cold suppers, or for any time. You can also serve them fried, baked, creamed, or sauced. But do serve them within two or three days. Contrary to general opinion, hard-cooked eggs do not keep. Refrigerate them away from raw eggs so that you do not become confused as to which is which.

Chop hard-cooked eggs. Use as garnish over creamed chicken or fish, mix in with cooked vegetables or green salads, or sprinkle over cold or hot broccoli or asparagus.

Spread thin slices of dark rye bread with soft butter. Cover with packed-in-mustard sardines. Cover sardines with sliced hard-cooked eggs, garnish with mayonnaise. Serve with dill pickle slices.

Spread dark rye bread with soft butter. Cover with slices of hard-cooked egg. Top egg slices with sour cream. Sprinkle with caviar.

Spread dark rye bread with mustard. Cover with thin slices of ripe tomatoes. Sprinkle tomatoes with chopped hard-cooked egg and chopped sweet red onion.

Spread thin slices of light rye bread with soft butter. Cover with slice of liver pâté. Cover pâté with chopped hard-cooked egg mixed with mustard and mayonnaise.

Spread melba toast rounds with soft butter, place a slice

of hard-cooked egg in the center, surround with caviar. Garnish egg slice with mayonnaise.

Cut hard-cooked egg in half. Place 2 halves in small ramekin. Cover with mayonnaise mixed with Roquefort cheese, mayonnaise mixed with chili sauce, or with chopped chives and freshly ground black pepper. Serve as appetizer.

Split hard-cooked eggs in half lengthwise. Remove yolks and stuff with:

Mashed egg yolks, chopped cooked shrimp, mayonnaise and chopped parsley, salt and pepper.

Mashed egg yolks, sweet butter, mashed sardines (poached in olive oil), lemon juice, salt and pepper.

Mashed egg yolks, sweet butter, red caviar, chopped parsley, salt and pepper.

Mashed egg yolks, cream cheese, Escoffier Sauce Robert (commercially bottled), chopped sweet pickles, salt and pepper.

Mashed egg yolks, sour cream, caviar, chopped onion.

Mashed egg yolks, heavy cream, minced chives, mustard, salt and pepper.

CURRIED HARD-COOKED EGGS
WITH RICE AND CHUTNEY

3 *tablespoons butter*	6 *hard-cooked eggs, sliced*
1 *tablespoon chopped shallots*	*Freshly cooked steamy hot*
2 *tablespoons flour*	*white rice*
½ *to* 1 *teaspoon curry powder*	*Grated coconut*
2 *cups light cream*	*Bombay duck*
¼ *cup chopped pimiento*	*Chutney (commercially*
Salt ⎱ *to taste* *Pepper* ⎰	*bottled)*

Melt butter in a heavy saucepan. Add shallots and cook, stirring, for 1 minute. Stir in flour and curry powder. When these are blended in, slowly add cream, blend, and cook, stirring, until sauce thickens. Add pimiento and season with salt and pepper. Add egg slices. Continue to cook only until egg slices are thoroughly heated.

To serve: Place cooked rice on oval serving platter. Spoon curried eggs and sauce over rice. Sprinkle surface with coconut and Bombay duck. Serve chutney separately.
[4 *servings*.]

HOT GOURMET SANDWICH
WITH HARD-COOKED EGGS

6 *hard-cooked eggs, chopped*
Warm cheese sauce
   (*see page* 81)
6 *slices white bread*

1 *small can deviled ham*
½ *cup shredded Swiss cheese*
Paprika

Combine eggs and Mornay sauce. Toast bread lightly. Spread with deviled ham. Cover with egg-sauce mixture. Sprinkle with cheese and paprika. Place under broiler, heat until lightly browned.
[*Makes 6 sandwiches.*]

MUSHROOM-EGG CROQUETTES

3 *tablespoons butter*
3 *tablespoons flour*
1 *cup milk*
2 *tablespoons dry sherry*
¼ *teaspoon salt*
4 *hard-cooked eggs, chopped*
1 *small can "sautéed in butter"*
   chopped mushrooms

¼ *cup chopped blanched*
   almonds

Flour
1 *egg, lightly beaten with 1*
   tablespoon water
1 *cup fine dry bread crumbs*
Oil for frying

Melt butter in saucepan. Add flour and blend until smooth. Slowly add milk, stirring it into the flour-butter mixture as it is added. Add sherry and cook, stirring, until sauce thickens. Season with salt. Remove from heat, add eggs, mushrooms, and almonds. Spread out on a lightly buttered platter. Refrigerate until well chilled. Dust hands with flour and shape mixture into small croquettes. Dip each into beaten egg, then roll in bread crumbs. Refrigerate until chilled.

Fill deep saucepan with oil to within 2 or 3 inches of rim. Heat to 375° on deep fat thermometer. Add croquettes and fry, a few at a time, until lightly browned. Drain on paper toweling. Serve with tomato or cream sauce.

[4 *servings.*]

HAM-STUFFED BAKED EGGS

8 *hard-cooked eggs*
¼ *cup butter*
1 *cup finely minced cooked*
  ham
3 *tablespoons dry sherry*
Salt
Freshly ground } *to taste*
  black pepper

2 *tablespoons flour*
1½ *cups milk*
1 *small can sliced "sautéed in*
  butter" mushrooms
Grated Swiss cheese

Cut the eggs in half lengthwise. Remove the yolks. Reserve whites. Mash yolks with half of the butter. Add ham and 1 tablespoon of the sherry, season lightly with salt and pepper, blend, and use to stuff whites. Place stuffed eggs close together in a small shallow baking dish.

Melt the remaining butter in a saucepan. Stir in the flour. When flour is blended in, slowly add the milk, stirring it into the flour mixture as it is added. Cook, stirring, over moderate heat until sauce is thick and smooth. Add the mushrooms and the remaining sherry and cook for 2 or 3 minutes longer. Then pour sauce over the stuffed eggs. Sprinkle surface with grated cheese and place dish under broiler heat until topping is lightly browned. Serve at once.

[4 *servings.*]

ALMOND EGG YOLK SAUCE

½ *cup almonds, blanched and*
toasted
3 *yolks of hard-cooked eggs*
Pinch of marjoram
1½ *cups canned or homemade*
chicken stock or broth
(*see page* 203)

Salt
Freshly ground ⎱ *to taste*
black pepper ⎰
2 *tablespoons minced parsley*

Place almonds, egg yolks, marjoram, and ½ cup stock in electric blender. Blend to a purée. Combine with remaining stock. Cook, stirring, over low heat until sauce is smooth and thick. Season to taste with salt and pepper. Add minced parsley at the last minute. Serve over chicken or fish.

[*Makes about* 1½ *cups sauce.*]

Breads, Cakes, and Such

Breads, Cakes, and Such

LEFTOVER BREADS, rolls, cakes, and such are not to be thought of lightly. Many of the world's great recipes were devised from these "too good to allow to go to waste" foods.

Store all plain cakes, cookies, muffins, and breads in airtight plastic bags in the freezer or in the freezing compartment of your refrigerator. They will stay fresh-baked up to six months. Freeze cakes with butter or cream frosting unwrapped. When very firm, wrap and store in freezer. Do not attempt to freeze cakes with boiled icing; frosting becomes sticky and will not freeze. Cakes with such icing should be kept covered in a cool dry place. Uncut, the icing will keep the cake fresh for two or three days. Once cut, they should be eaten.

Crumbs

ONE OF THE BEST and most obvious ways to use up that last bit of cake, those few cookies, or the end of that loaf of French bread is, of course, to make bread crumbs.

Crumbs made from homemade cakes and good bread from a fine bakery are far better than those you buy in a package and cost less. And if you make them from stale bread or cake that would otherwise be thrown out, you can discount the entire cost. Stored in an airtight container in your freezer or in the freezing compartment of your refrigerator, they will stay fresh up to six months.

MADE-IN-A-BLENDER BREAD CRUMBS

1 *slice bread = about ½ cup crumbs*

Tear bread into 5 or 6 pieces, blend at low speed to desired consistency.

BUTTERED BREAD CRUMBS

Spread bread with butter before placing in blender.

CHEESE CRUMBS

Add a few small cubes of hard cheese to bread before blending.

HERB CRUMBS

Add a pinch, or more, of dried herbs to bread before blending.

CRUMBS SANS A BLENDER

Use stale bread, grate in old-fashioned grater. If bread is soft, dry out in a very low (250°) oven before grating.

ITALIAN SEASONED CRUMBS

1 *cup bread crumbs*
¼ *teaspoon salt*
⅛ *teaspoon pepper*

¼ *teaspoon oregano* (*crush leaves before adding*)
⅛ *teaspoon Beau Monde seasoning*

Blend all ingredients well and refrigerate crumbs in air-tight container. Use as needed.

COOKIE CRUMBS

8 *blended-in-a-blender wafer-type cookies* = *about* 1 *cup crumbs*

Use as you would packaged crumbs, but of course for far less money.

Roll small balls of pistachio ice cream in chocolate cookie crumbs. Freeze until very firm. Place by threes in individual dessert bowls. Spoon Melba sauce (commercially bottled) over surface. Garnish with whipped cream. Or, do the same with vanilla wafer crumbs, strawberry ice cream, and fresh strawberries; macaroon crumbs, chocolate ice cream, and chocolate sauce; and so on, ad infinitum.

Mix cookie crumbs—any kind—with sweetened whipped cream generously laced with cognac, other brandy, or rum. Drop by spoonfuls onto flat tray. Freeze until firm, then store in plastic bag in freezer. Serve as a glamour dessert to un-expected—*or* expected—guests. Great with small cups of black coffee.

Or, mix cookie crumbs with sour cream. Spoon over fresh fruit or stewed fruit or even canned fruit. Elegant over brandied peaches.

BREAD SAUCE

¼ cup shallots or scallions, chopped
2 cups milk
1 clove
½ cup bread crumbs, made from fresh bread (crust removed)

1 tablespoon butter
Salt
Freshly ground black pepper } to taste

Combine shallots or scallions, milk, and clove in saucepan. Bring to boil, lower heat, and simmer gently for 5 minutes. Strain. Add bread crumbs and cook, stirring, until sauce is smooth. Add butter and seasoning. Use as you would any white sauce.

[*Makes about 2½ cups sauce.*]

POLONAISE SAUCE

6 tablespoons butter
4 tablespoons fine dry bread crumbs
2 tablespoons finely chopped parsley

1 tablespoon lemon juice
Salt
Pepper } to taste

Place butter in a heavy skillet over low heat and cook until it begins to brown. Add bread crumbs and cook, stirring, until they are lightly browned. Stir in parsley and lemon juice. Season to taste with salt and pepper.

Serve over fish or vegetables.

[*Makes about ½ cup sauce.*]

SWISS CHEESE AND BREAD SOUP

4 *thick slices of stale French or*   4 *cups milk*
    Italian-style bread   *Salt* ⎰
Butter   *Pepper* ⎱ *to taste*
1 *cup grated Swiss cheese*   *Freshly grated nutmeg*

Spread each slice of bread generously with butter. Place each in an individual ovenproof soup tureen. Place tureens in 350° oven until butter has melted. Sprinkle ¼ cup cheese over each slice of bread.

Heat milk until steamy hot. Pour over bread and cheese. Sprinkle with salt, pepper, and nutmeg. Serve at once.
[4 *servings.*]

BREAD CRUMB GRIDDLE CAKES

1½ *cups fine dry bread crumbs*   2 *teaspoons baking powder*
1½ *cups milk, scalded*   ⅛ *teaspoon salt*
2 *tablespoons melted butter*   2 *eggs, well beaten*
½ *cup flour*   *Maple syrup*

Combine bread crumbs with milk and butter.

Sift flour with baking powder and salt. Add egg, blend, and combine with bread crumb and milk mixture.

Heat griddle until a drop of water sputters on its surface. Pour or spoon batter onto griddle to make 2- to 3-inch cakes. Cook each griddle cake until surface bubbles and underside is lightly browned. Turn and brown second side.

Serve with warm maple syrup.
[4 *to* 6 *servings.*]

MEXICAN CHEESE CAKE

8 *slices stale sponge cake*
4 *tablespoons butter*
1½ *cups sugar*
1½ *cups water*
¼ *cup cognac or other good brandy*

4 *eggs, separated*
½ *lb. soft Monterey Jack cheese, crumbled*
½ *teaspoon cinnamon*

Cut cake slices into small squares. Heat 2 tablespoons of the butter in a heavy saucepan. Add the cake slices and fry until lightly browned. Remove from pan and set aside.

Combine sugar and water in saucepan. Bring to boil, lower heat, and simmer for 5 minutes. Remove from heat and add cognac.

Beat egg yolks in mixing bowl. Add brandy syrup in slow stream, beating constantly. Beat the egg whites until stiff and fold them into the yolk mixture. Add cinnamon.

Line a 2-quart buttered shallow baking dish with wax paper. Butter paper with remaining 2 tablespoons butter. Cover with half of the cake squares. Sprinkle with half of the crumbled cheese. Cover with half of the syrup-egg mixture. Repeat. Bake in 325° oven until firm—about 30 minutes. Serve warm with ice cream or whipped cream.

[6 *to 8 servings.*]

MEXICAN CONVENT SUNDAY DESSERT

1½ *cups sugar*
1½ *cups water*
½ *cup peach or apricot brandy*
8 *slices stale pound cake*

5 *egg yolks, lightly beaten*
¼ *cup slivered almonds*
2 *brandied peaches, sliced*

Combine sugar and water in top half of double boiler. Place over direct heat and bring to boil. Boil for 3 minutes, remove from heat, and stir in brandy.

Place cake slices on dessert plates. Moisten each with a little of the brandy syrup.

Slowly add egg yolks to remaining syrup, beating constantly. Place over simmering water and cook, stirring, until mixture coats the spoon. Pour over cake slices. Sprinkle each serving with almonds and garnish with peach slices. Serve warm. [8 *servings.*]

EARLY AMERICAN BREAD PUDDING

2 *cups soft large bread crumbs*
½ *cup all-purpose flour*
¾ *cup brown sugar*
½ *cup finely diced candied*
  orange and lemon peel
¼ *cup butter, melted and*
  cooled

2 *whole eggs*
3 *egg yolks*
⅛ *teaspoon cinnamon*
⅛ *teaspoon nutmeg*
¼ *cup rum*

Combine bread crumbs, flour, brown sugar, candied peel, and melted butter in large mixing bowl. Beat whole eggs with egg yolks, cinnamon, and nutmeg. Add rum. Pour over bread mixture and blend well. Pour into a well-buttered 1½- or 2-quart baking dish. Place in a large pan of hot water. Bake in a preheated 375° oven until firm (about 30 minutes).

Serve with hot custard sauce flavored with rum (see page 168).
[6 *to* 8 *servings.*]

FRENCH CABINET PUDDING

½ *cup mixed candied fruit*
½ *cup seedless raisins*
⅓ *cup kirsch*
4 *cups milk*
2 *tablespoons butter*
1 *cup sugar*
5 *whole eggs*

4 *egg yolks*
1 *teaspoon vanilla*
8 *to* 10 *slices stale French*
  bread, torn into small cubes
  (enough to make about 2
  cups bread)
Confectioners' sugar

Combine candied fruit, raisins, and kirsch. Set aside. Place milk in saucepan and bring almost to a boil. Remove from heat, add butter and sugar. Stir until butter has melted. Beat whole eggs with egg yolks in a large mixing bowl. Stir milk mixture into eggs. Add vanilla.

Butter a 2-quart baking dish. Add the bread cubes, candied fruit, raisins, and kirsch. Pour the custard mixture over the surface. Place the baking dish in a large pan of hot water and bake in a preheated 375° oven until firm (35 to 45 minutes). Sprinkle surface with confectioners' sugar and place under broiler heat until glazed.

[8 *to* 10 *servings.*]

CHOCOLATE BREAD PUDDING

4 *cups milk*	2 *whole eggs*
1 *cup sugar*	2 *egg yolks*
2 *cups bread crumbs*	1 *tablespoon dark rum, or, as*
2 *1-oz. squares chocolate*	*substitute, 1 teaspoon vanilla*

Place milk in saucepan, bring almost to a boil. Remove from heat, add sugar, and pour over bread crumbs in mixing bowl.

Melt the chocolate in top of double boiler over simmering water. Remove from heat and add ½ cup of the milk from the bread and milk mixture. Add the whole eggs, egg yolks, and rum (or vanilla). Blend well and combine with the remaining bread and milk mixture. Pour into a 2-quart baking dish and place dish in a large pan of warm water. Bake in preheated 375° oven until firm—about 45 minutes.

[6 *to* 8 *servings.*]

BLACKBERRY BREAD PUDDING

3 *cups fresh blackberries*
½ *cup water*
1 *cup sugar*
Butter

8 *to* 10 *slices of stale bread,*
    crust removed
2 *egg whites*

Combine berries and water in saucepan. Cook over low heat for 10 minutes. Add ¾ cup of the sugar. Butter each bread slice. Cut each in 3 strips.

Line a buttered baking dish with some of the bread slices, butter side up. Spoon some of the berries over the surface. Repeat until all berries and bread have been used, ending with berries.

Beat egg whites until stiff, fold in remaining sugar, beat to a stiff meringue. Spoon over surface of berries. Place in a preheated 450° oven until meringue is lightly browned. Refrigerate until well chilled.
[6 *servings.*]

NOTE: Sliced fresh strawberries or any other berries may be substituted for blackberries.

STALE-CAKE PUDDING

¾ *cup mixed candied fruit*
½ *cup seedless raisins*
¼ *cup Grand Marnier*
2 *cups milk*
¾ *cup sugar*

2 *cups stale-cake crumbs*
    (*sponge cake, white or yellow cake, layer cake*)
3 *eggs, lightly beaten*
Apricot sauce (*see page* 140)

Combine candied fruit, raisins, and Grand Marnier. Set aside. Place milk in large saucepan, bring almost to boil. Remove from heat and stir in sugar. Add cake crumbs, lightly beaten eggs, and candied fruit, raisins, and any liqueur that has not soaked into the fruit. Blend and pour into a buttered 2-quart baking dish. Place in a large pan of warm water

and bake in a preheated 375° oven until firm (30 to 40 minutes). Serve with apricot sauce.
[6 *to* 8 *servings.*]

POUDING AU PAIN À L'ALLEMANDE
(German Bread Pudding)

¼ *cup finely diced candied orange peel*
½ *cup raisins*
2 *cups (dry white) Rhine wine*
3 *cups soft bread crumbs*
¾ *cup brown sugar*

⅛ *teaspoon cinnamon*
2 *whole eggs* ⎫
3 *egg yolks* ⎬ *lightly beaten*
½ *cup (1 stick) butter, melted and cooled*
3 *egg whites*

Combine orange peel and raisins. Add ½ cup of the wine. Let stand for 30 minutes. Combine remaining wine with bread crumbs, brown sugar, and cinnamon. Let stand for 30 minutes. Then purée this mixture in an electric blender or force through a fine sieve. Add whole eggs, egg yolks, and melted (cooled) butter. Blend well and fold in orange peel and raisins. Beat egg whites until stiff, fold into bread mixture. Pour into a 2-quart soufflé or pudding mold, place mold in a large pan of warm water. Bake in a preheated 375° oven until firm and lightly browned—about 30 minutes.
[6 *to* 8 *servings.*]

But What Do I Do With...?

Anchovies

If oil from can has been used or discarded, cover leftover anchovies with a small amount of salad oil. Store in airtight container in refrigerator.

To use 2 to 4 leftover anchovies, drain, then snip with kitchen shears into green salads, mixed vegetable salads, tomato sauce for spaghetti, or cream sauce for vegetables.

Cut into small pieces, then mash with fork to a paste. Blend into mayonnaise or add to French dressing.

Slice anchovies lengthwise. Use as garnish for poached eggs, boiled potatoes, or individual servings of boiled vegetables.

ANCHOVY BUTTER

Cut 6 anchovies into small pieces. Mash to a smooth paste, blend into ½ cup (1 stick) soft (room temperature) butter. Use as spread for canapés or sandwiches, or use as topping for just-broiled steak (1 pat, about 1 teaspoon, anchovy butter per steak). Anchovy butter may be stored in refrigerator or freezer, to be used as needed.

ENSALADA DE BOQUERON Y ACEITUNA
(Spanish Olive and Anchovy Salad)

Combine 4 minced anchovy fillets, 2 minced pimientos, ¼ cup olive oil, 2 tablespoons red wine vinegar, ¼ teaspoon salt, and a pinch of cumin with ½ cup diced stuffed green

olives. Blend well. Add to approximately 4 cups mixed greens: romaine, Boston lettuce, crisp young spinach leaves, escarole, etc. Toss lightly.
[6 *to* 8 *servings.*]

Chocolate Milk, Cocoa, or Hot Chocolate

REFRIGERATE in empty (rinsed out with cold water) milk carton. Use within two or three days, in place of plain milk in recipes also using chocolate or cocoa.

Coconut—Fresh

GRATE AND FREEZE leftover portions of fresh coconut. Store in freezer in small airtight container. Defrost for 15 to 20 minutes at room temperature before using.

COCONUT MILK

Pour boiling water over coconut (fresh or frozen). Let stand for 30 minutes. Drain. Use to make cream curry sauce, custard, pudding, cake, or cookies.

Place leftover coconut on flat pan. Toast in a 300° oven until lightly browned. Use for cooking or as garnish.

Coffee

NEVER, but never, attempt to reheat leftover coffee. Use it instead to make frozen cubes for iced coffee. Simply pour cold coffee into ice cube tray; when cubes are firm, eject them and store in plastic bag in freezer. Use as needed.

Substitute part cold leftover coffee for milk in making chocolate cakes, cookies, custards, and puddings—gives a lovely mocha flavor.

MOCHA SAUCE

2 1-oz. squares unsweetened chocolate
6 tablespoons cold leftover coffee
½ cup sugar
3 tablespoons butter
¼ teaspoon vanilla

Place chocolate and coffee in top of double boiler. Cook over simmering water until blended. Add sugar and butter, stir until dissolved. Blend until smooth, remove from heat and stir in vanilla. Serve hot or cold.
[*Makes about 1 cup sauce.*]

COFFEE GELATIN PARFAIT

2 envelopes unflavored gelatin
½ cup cold water
3 cups cold leftover coffee
¾ cup sugar
½ cup coffee liqueur
1 cup heavy cream

Sprinkle gelatin over cold water in top of double boiler. Place over simmering water and stir until gelatin is dissolved. Add coffee and ½ cup of the sugar, stir until sugar has dissolved. Remove from heat and add ¼ cup of the coffee liqueur. Pour into shallow pan and refrigerate until firm.

Whip cream with remaining sugar until stiff. Fold in remaining liqueur. Cut chilled, firm gelatin into small cubes. Spoon about half of these into the bottom of 6 parfait glasses, cover with some of the whipped cream, add a second layer of diced gelatin, and top with remaining whipped cream. [6 *servings*.]

Dill Pickles

GLAZE THEM. Combine ¾ cup sugar and ½ cup tarragon vinegar in saucepan. Stir over low heat until sugar dissolves. Add dill pickles, cut lengthwise into thin strips. Simmer for 5 to 10 minutes. Place in jar, cover, and refrigerate until chilled.

Gravy

FREEZE IT in ice cube trays; when gravy is frozen, eject cubes and store in plastic bag in freezer. Reheat slowly. Pour over quick-cooked meats for slow-cooked flavor. Add frozen to hot stews, sauces, soup—or gravy.

Lemonade

POUR INTO ICE CUBE TRAYS and freeze. Eject cubes when firm and store in plastic bag in freezer. Great with iced tea instead of plain ice; or, use in fruit punch.

Marshmallows

TO KEEP THEM FROM DRYING OUT, store in plastic bag in freezer. Cut with kitchen shears while still frozen. Use—but everyone knows how to use marshmallows.

Olives

DRAIN those last few ripe or green olives and cover with French dressing. Add a split clove of garlic to the jar, cover, and refrigerate. Unless you are a real garlic fan, remove the garlic after two or three days. Olives will stay fresh indefinitely.

Cut ripe green olives into slivers. Blend into cream sauce. Adds color and a flavor plus.

Chop pimiento-stuffed green olives. Add to mayonnaise.

Wrap large pitted black olives in bacon. Broil until bacon is crisp.

Slice pimiento-stuffed green olives. Heat in butter. Pour over just-broiled fish.

Mix a 3-oz. package of cream cheese with 3 tablespoons sour cream. Add ¼ cup slivered black olives. Stir into just-cooked chopped spinach (fresh or frozen). Heat briefly and serve. (A good sauce for any vegetable.)

OLIVE SPREAD FOR CANAPÉS

8 *to* 12 *large ripe olives, pitted*   3 *tablespoons brandy*
4 *to* 6 *anchovy fillets*   1 *3-oz. package cream cheese*
1 *teaspoon Dijon mustard*   2 *tablespoons milk or cream*

Place all ingredients in electric blender, blend to a smooth spread.
Or, place olives and anchovy fillets in a wooden bowl. Pound to a smooth paste and combine with remaining ingredients.
[*Makes about* 1 *cup spread.*]

Parsley

IF PARSLEY WAS FRESH when purchased, it will keep fresh in the refrigerator for a week or more if thoroughly washed, then stored in a widemouthed jar or small pitcher with the stems in water (rather like a small bunch of flowers). Cover parsley and jar with a plastic bag sealed to jar with a rubber band.

If you would keep parsley for a month or two, freeze it. Wash thoroughly, pat dry with paper toweling, remove tough stems, and chop very fine. Store in small containers in freezer. Use frozen.

Any fresh herb may be frozen and stored in the same way.

Pimientos

To STORE that leftover half jar of pimientos, add a teaspoon of vinegar to remaining liquid. Cover jar and refrigerate. Or, if no liquid remains, cover pimientos completely with cold water. Cover jar and refrigerate.

To use 2 or 3 leftover pimientos, you might snip them with kitchen shears into sauces, soups, or stews. Use as a garnish for vegetables, add to a green salad, to mayonnaise or French dressing. Toss with hot cooked rice or pasta.

Or, dice very fine and cream into cream cheese or soft cheddar. Add to scrambled eggs or omelets.

Potato Chips

LEAVE CHIPS in original cellophane bag and place inside plastic bag. Store in freezer. Recrisp in 250° oven before serving.

Tea

FREEZE LEFTOVER TEA in ice cube trays. When cubes are firm, eject them and store in plastic bag in freezer. Use instead of plain ice cubes for iced tea, or make:

TEA PUNCH

6 to 8 sprigs fresh mint, chopped, stems removed
1/4 cup sugar
1 cup fresh orange juice
1/4 cup fresh lemon juice
2 cups strong cold tea
3/4 cup tea-flavored brandy
2 quarts sparkling water
Tea ice cubes

Place chopped mint in mortar or in wooden bowl. Add sugar and pound with pestle or with heavy wooden spoon until mint is well crushed into sugar. Combine orange juice, lemon juice, tea, and tea brandy. Add the crushed mint and sugar. Stir until sugar has dissolved. Pour into punch bowl. Add sparkling water and tea ice cubes.
[Makes about 3 quarts punch.]

Turkey Stuffing

SPREAD THIN SLICES of white bread with soft butter, cover with thin slices of cold turkey stuffing, top each with thin slice of cranberry jelly and second slice of buttered bread.

Or, heat leftover turkey stuffing with leftover bits of turkey and turkey gravy. Pile onto toasted hamburger buns that have been spread with cranberry jelly—another version of a Sloppy Joe.

Watermelon—The Leftover Half

IT WON'T KEEP more than a day or two unless you make:

WATERMELON ICE

½ large watermelon (enough   ¼ cup fresh lemon juice
  to make about 4 cups juice)   ¾ cup sugar
1 cup fresh orange juice   2 egg whites

Remove rind and seeds from watermelon. Press through a sieve to extract juice or place in electric blender and blend until liquefied.

Add to watermelon juice the orange and lemon juice and ½ cup of the sugar. Pour into ice cube trays and freeze to mushy stage.

Beat egg whites until stiff, beat in remaining sugar.

Place partially frozen watermelon mixture in chilled bowl and fold in beaten egg whites. Transfer to a large mold or soufflé dish. Cover mold or dish with foil and place in freezer until firm.

[6 to 8 servings.]

Sandwiches

WRAP LEFTOVER SANDWICHES in a napkin that has been wrung out in ice water. Cover with foil. Refrigerate. They will remain fresh for two to three days.

Or, you may wrap sandwiches in foil and store in freezer, but only if spread with butter, not mayonnaise (mayonnaise curdles), and made without tomato slices and lettuce.

For a change in taste, French fry yesterday's sandwiches:

FRENCH FRIED SANDWICHES

3 *eggs, lightly beaten*
3 *tablespoons water*
2 *tablespoons salad oil*
Dash of salt

3 *to 4 leftover sandwiches (any filling, white or light brown bread)*
4 *tablespoons vegetable oil*
2 *tablespoons butter*

Beat eggs with water, salad oil, and salt, pour into shallow pan. Holding sandwiches firmly together, dip them in the egg mixture, first on one side, then on the other.

Heat the oil with the butter in a heavy skillet. Add sandwiches and fry until golden brown on both sides. Transfer to a shallow baking pan and place in a preheated 350° oven for about 5 minutes. Drain briefly on paper toweling before serving.

[*Makes 3 or 4 fried sandwiches.*]

Basic Recipes for Leftovers

Basic Recipes for Leftovers

MOST OF US KNOW one of those very good cooks who can whip up a meal from what's on hand without even a glance at a cookbook—or maybe that good cook is you. If so, you will undoubtedly be familiar with one or more variations of the recipes to follow.

These are the "basics" for leftover cookery—extenders all, and adaptable to a variety of ingredients. But more than that, of course, they are also the base for many classic gourmet dishes, and have been proven worth the effort by generations of very good cooks.

Stock

WHO MAKES HOMEMADE STOCK these days when clear broth and consommé come so conveniently canned and ready to use? Two types of people do—people who insist on superb flavor, and people who are concerned with the nutritional value of food.

Homemade stock is one of the simple secrets of truly great cuisine. It adds a rich taste and texture to soup, stew, and sauce that can be obtained in no other way.

It also has the homey virtue of supplying an abundance of minerals and vitamins not to be found in commercial substitutes.

Obviously it is the ideal base for dishes made from leftovers. How you feel about taking the time to prepare homemade stock depends on how strongly you feel about the flavor and quality of the food that you serve.

Certainly, making stock takes no special skill. What's more, once made, it may be frozen and used as needed week after week, with no more effort than it takes to open that can.

BEEF STOCK

½ lb. beef (chuck, plate, or flanken)
2 beef marrow bones
1 beef knuckle
1 veal knuckle
5 quarts water (approximately)
1½ teaspoons salt
6 to 8 peppercorns

1 large onion, stuck with 3 cloves
2 stalks celery, with leaves
2 carrots, scraped
1 large leek
2 sprigs parsley
1 bay leaf
1 clove garlic (optional)

Place meat, marrow bones, and knuckles in large soup kettle. Brown on all sides over medium heat (do not add oil or shortening). Add water and bring to boil. Lower heat and skim foam from surface. Continue skimming until foam ceases to rise. Add remaining ingredients. Cover partially and simmer over very low heat for 4 to 5 hours. Remove meat and bones. Strain stock and pour into nonmetal container. Refrigerate until fat rises to the surface and congeals. Remove fat. Seal container with foil. Transfer to freezer. Store frozen until ready to use.

Reheat and use in making leftover dishes, or use in making brown sauce. Use in any recipe calling for beef gravy.

Substitute for water in cooking rice, pasta, or vegetables. Use as base for meat sauce.

NOTE: Use meat to make hash, or simply slice and serve as you would any boiled beef.

CHICKEN STOCK

1 5- to 6-lb. chicken, cut up for sautéing
4 quarts water (approximately)
2 teaspoons salt
5 allspice berries
¼ teaspoon freshly ground black pepper

2 stalks celery, with leaves
1 bay leaf
2 leeks, sliced
3 sprigs parsley
2 medium tomatoes, quartered
1 medium onion, quartered

Place chicken in large soup kettle. Cover with water, bring to boil. Lower heat and skim foam from surface. Continue skimming until foam ceases to rise. Add remaining ingredients, cover partially, and simmer for 2 to 2½ hours, or until fowl is tender. Remove chicken. Simmer stock for an additional ½ hour. Strain into container. Refrigerate until fat rises to the surface and congeals. Remove fat. Seal container with foil. Freeze and store in freezer until ready to use.

Reheat and serve as clear soup. Use in any recipe calling for canned chicken stock or broth. Substitute for water in cooking rice, pasta, or vegetables. Use as base for chicken gravy or substitute for ¼ to 1 cup milk in making cream sauce.

[*Makes about 6 quarts.*]

NOTE: Use the chicken itself in any recipes calling for boiled chicken (see chicken chapter).

CHICKEN GRAVY

2 tablespoons minced shallots
2 tablespoons butter or chicken fat

1 tablespoon flour
1½ cups chicken stock

Sauté shallots in butter or chicken fat in heavy skillet until they are limp but not browned. Stir in flour. Cook over very low heat, stirring constantly with wooden spoon, until flour turns a deep golden brown. Slowly add chicken stock, stirring it into the flour mixture as it is added. Cook, stirring frequently, until gravy is thick and smooth. Serve over sautéed, fried, or baked chicken.

[*Makes about 1½ cups gravy.*]

ASPIC FOR MEAT OR POULTRY

2½ cups beef or chicken stock
1 tablespoon chopped celery
   leaves
1 tablespoon chopped green
   onion
1 egg white, lightly beaten
1 egg shell, crumbled
1 envelope unflavored gelatin
½ cup Madeira, sherry, or
   port
Salt, to taste

Combine stock, celery leaves, green onion, egg white, and egg shell in saucepan. Place over low heat, simmer gently for 20 minutes. Remove from heat.

Sprinkle gelatin over Madeira or other wine. Let stand for 5 minutes. Then add to hot stock and stir until dissolved. Let stock stand for 20 minutes at room temperature, then strain through a triple thickness of cheesecloth. Season with salt to taste.

If aspic thickens before you are ready to use it, reheat briefly.

Use in making jellied meat, poultry, or vegetable salads or molds.

[*Makes about 2 cups.*]

GLAZE FOR COLD MEAT OR POULTRY

Prepare basic aspic. Refrigerate until it starts to congeal. Brush over very cold sliced meat or poultry (or poultry pieces) on chilled platter. Use two or more coats, letting each coat congeal before adding the next. Refrigerate until ready to serve. Pour remaining aspic into a shallow pan. Refrigerate until firm. Dice, or use a fork to "scramble." Use as garnish for aspic-glazed meat or poultry platter.

Sauces

BROWN SAUCE

A quick version of the classic French sauce Espagnole or brown sauce. Used instead of canned beef gravy, it makes the difference between "just good" and "truly great." Canned consommé or broth may be substituted for stock, but again "homemade" flavor is lost.

2 *tablespoons butter*
1 *tablespoon flour*
2 *cups beef stock*
Salt ⎫
Pepper ⎭ *to taste*

1 *or* 2 *tablespoons cognac or other good brandy* (*optional*)

Melt butter in saucepan over moderate heat. Stir in flour and cook, stirring, until flour turns a light brown. Stir in stock and cook, stirring, until sauce thickens. Season to taste with salt and pepper. Add cognac, blend, and serve.
[*Makes about 2 cups sauce.*]

MADEIRA SAUCE

Prepare basic brown sauce. Add ½ cup madeira, blend, and cook, stirring frequently, until sauce again thickens.

MUSHROOM SAUCE

½ lb. mushrooms, thinly sliced   ½ cup dry red wine
2 tablespoons butter   2 tablespoons sour cream
1 tablespoon flour   Salt ⎫
1 cup beef stock   Pepper ⎭ to taste

Sauté mushrooms in butter in heavy saucepan. Stir in flour; when flour is lightly browned, slowly add stock and blend with wire whisk until smooth. Add wine. Cook, stirring, until sauce thickens. Stir in sour cream. Season to taste with salt and pepper. Blend and serve.
[*Makes about 2 cups sauce.*]

NOTE: Heavy cream may be substituted for sour cream if desired.

SAUCE DIABLE

2 tablespoons chopped onion   2 to 3 dashes Tabasco sauce
1 tablespoon butter   Salt ⎫
1 tablespoon flour   Freshly ground ⎬ to taste
⅓ cup dry white wine   black pepper ⎭
1 cup beef stock
1 tablespoon Worcestershire
   sauce

Sauté onion in butter in heavy saucepan until limp. Add flour and stir until lightly browned. Stir in wine, blend, and add beef stock and seasonings. Cook, stirring, until sauce thickens.
[*Makes about 1½ cups sauce.*]

SAUCE CHASSEUR
(Hunter's Sauce)

Prepare basic brown sauce. Add ⅓ cup dry white wine, ¼ cup chopped shallots, and 1 tablespoon tomato paste. Blend and cook, stirring, until thoroughly heated.

CREAM SAUCE

Who needs a recipe for simple cream sauce? If one were to judge from a number of sad experiences, it seems that quite a few would-be good cooks still do.

BASIC CREAM SAUCE

2 *tablespoons butter*   ¼ *teaspoon salt*
1 *tablespoon flour*   *Sprinkling of white pepper*
1¼ *cups milk*

Heat butter in a heavy saucepan. Stir in flour. When flour is blended in, slowly add milk, stirring with a wire whisk. Cook, stirring, over low heat until sauce thickens. Season to taste with salt and pepper.
[*Makes about* 1 *cup.*]

SOME DOS AND DON'TS

Do use a heavy saucepan. If you don't have one, make your sauce in a double boiler over simmering water. Do not allow water to touch bottom of upper pan.

Do use low heat when melting butter. Do not allow butter to brown. Keep heat low while blending in flour. Do not allow flour to brown.

Cook sauce slowly. Stir with wire whisk. Cook until no trace of starchy taste remains.

MEDIUM CREAM SAUCE

Increase flour to 2 tablespoons.

THICK CREAM SAUCE

Increase butter to 4 tablespoons, flour to 3 tablespoons.

VARIATIONS

Substitute ½ to 1 cup chicken stock for an equivalent amount of milk.

Substitute ½ cup white wine for an equivalent amount of milk.

Stir in 1 to 2 tablespoons good cognac, other brandy, or dry sherry just before serving.

Add ½ cup grated sharp cheese. Stir until blended.

Stir a little hot sauce into 2 well-beaten egg yolks, stir yolk mixture into rest of sauce, and remove from heat immediately.

Substitute ½ to 1 cup sour cream for an equivalent amount of milk. Stir in a little prepared horseradish just before serving.

Stir in 1 tablespoon tomato purée.

Add ¼ cup of any of the following:

Slivered almonds
Pimiento slivers
Sautéed-in-butter mushrooms
Ripe olive slivers
Thin slices of water chestnuts
Diced cooked shrimp
Julienne strips of baked or boiled ham
Chopped oysters
Chopped pimiento-stuffed green olives
Crisp garlicky buttered croutons (serve immediately, before they become soggy)

FRUIT SAUCE WITH ANY FRUIT JUICE

¾ *cup sugar*	1 *tablespoon water*
1 *cup any fresh, canned, or bottled fruit juice*	1 *tablespoon any desired liqueur (optional)*
1 *teaspoon cornstarch*	

Combine sugar and fruit juice in saucepan. Place over moderate heat and cook, stirring, until sugar has dissolved.

Combine cornstarch and water, blend until smooth; add to saucepan and stir until sauce is clear and thick. Remove from heat, add liqueur if desired. Serve hot or refrigerate and serve cold as needed.

[*Makes about 2 cups sauce.*]

Rice, Croquettes, and Fritters

PILAF

Basically easy to prepare, this rice dish from India and the Middle East has seemingly endless variations.

2 *tablespoons butter*
1 *cup short-grain Italian rice, or, as substitute, long-grain rice*
1 *small onion, finely chopped*
1 *clove garlic, finely minced*
½ *small green pepper, finely chopped*

3 *cups stock, chicken or beef*
Salt ⎱
Pepper ⎰ *to taste*
¾ *to 1 cup leftover cooked chicken, beef, pork, lamb, ham, shrimp, lobster, or flaked fish*

Heat butter in a heavy saucepan (one with a tight-fitting cover). Add the rice and stir over moderate heat until each grain is well coated and translucent. Add onion, garlic, and green pepper. Stir until vegetables are limp (do not allow vegetables or rice to brown).

Bring stock to boil in separate saucepan, season to taste with salt and pepper. Pour boiling stock over rice mixture.

Cover pan tightly and allow rice to simmer over low heat until it is tender and almost all the liquid has been absorbed (20 to 25 minutes). Fork-stir in chicken, meat, or fish. Cover

and cook until added ingredients are thoroughly heated and rice has absorbed all liquid.
[4 *to* 6 *servings.*]

NOTE: For extra flavor and interest, add about ¼ cup of any one or two of the following:
>   Chopped pine nuts
>   Slivered almonds
>   Seedless white raisins
>   Sautéed-in-butter mushrooms
>   Diced pimiento
>   Chopped Greek or Italian ripe olives
>   Cooked spicy Italian sausage
>   Thin, thin strips of green onion
>   Chopped scallions
>   Sliced pimiento-stuffed green olives

BASIC CROQUETTES

2 *cups diced chicken, seafood, ham, lamb, veal, or vegetables*
1½ *cups milk, or part milk, part clear chicken stock*
½ *cup butter*
½ *clove garlic* (*optional*)
1 *medium onion, chopped*
1 *teaspoon salt*

½ *cup flour*
2 *egg yolks, lightly beaten*
½ *cup flour*
1 *egg, beaten with* 1 *tablespoon milk,* 1 *tablespoon salad oil*
1 *cup fine dry bread crumbs*
Oil for deep frying

Place chicken, meat, seafood, or vegetables and half of milk in electric blender. Blend at high speed to a purée.

Melt butter in a large heavy saucepan, add garlic and onion. Cook, stirring, until onion is limp. Add salt and flour, blend until smooth. Add the puréed ingredients and remaining milk or stock; cook, stirring, until mixture is very thick. Remove from heat. Cool slightly, then quickly stir in the egg yolks. Pour into a long shallow pan and chill.

Shape the chilled mixture into small cones or cylinders. Roll them first in flour, then in the egg mixture, and finally in bread crumbs. Refrigerate until well chilled and firm (2 hours or longer).

Fry the croquettes in deep hot fat (360°), a few at a time, until lightly browned. Drain on paper toweling.

Serve plain as hors d'oeuvre, or serve with any appropriate sauce as an entree.

[8 *to* 10 *servings when made into small hors d'oeuvres;* 4 *servings as an entree.*]

FRITTER BATTER

1 *cup flour*	2 *eggs, lightly beaten*
½ *teaspoon salt*	¾ *cup beer*
3 *tablespoons butter, melted and cooled*	2 *egg whites, stiffly beaten*

Sift flour with salt into mixing bowl. Combine cooled butter with lightly beaten eggs. Stir into flour. Add the beer and blend only until batter is smooth.

Set batter aside at room temperature for 1 to 2 hours. Fold in stiffly beaten egg whites.

[*Makes enough batter for about* 3 *dozen small fritters.*]

TO FRY FRITTERS

Fill deep heavy pan with peanut or corn oil to within about 3 inches of rim. Heat to 360° on deep fat thermometer (or until small cube of soft white bread will brown in 35 seconds).

Use kitchen tongs or slotted spoon to dip small (bite-size) pieces of cooked food into batter. Meat, fowl, fish, or crisp-cooked vegetables may be used. Drop coated pieces into hot fat and fry a few at a time until lightly browned. Or, add chopped or minced cooked food and batter and drop by table-spoonfuls into hot fat. Fry portions, a few at a time, until lightly browned. Remove with slotted spoon and drain on paper toweling. Place on warm platter and keep warm until all fritters are made.

CORN FRITTERS

Add 1 cup leftover kernel corn and 2 or 3 chopped pimientos to fritter batter just before adding beaten egg whites.

HAM FRITTERS

Add ¾ cup finely diced or ground lean leftover cooked ham and ¼ cup well-drained finely chopped crisp sweet pickles to fritter batter just before adding beaten egg whites.

CHICKEN FRITTERS

Add 1 cup finely diced or ground leftover cooked chicken and 1 tablespoon minced parsley to fritter batter just before adding beaten egg whites.

SEAFOOD FRITTERS

Add 1 cup finely diced or flaked cooked shrimp, lobster, or other salt-water fish, ⅛ teaspoon thyme, and 1 tablespoon lemon juice to fritter batter just before adding beaten egg whites.

Crêpes

GOSSAMER light and paper thin, crêpes are the never-failing answer for the gourmet cook. Filled with leftover creamed chicken, diced meat in rich sauce, creamed shrimp, lobster, or just about any fruit of the sea, they make an elegant luncheon or late supper dish, an hors d'oeuvre worth remembering, or an impressive "after the soup course" for the most formal of seated meals.

With a little practice, they are simplicity itself to make, and what's more—though certainly it's no news to the professional chef—they can be made ahead, refrigerated or frozen, then reheated with almost no effort and certainly no last-minute kitchen confusion.

BASIC CRÊPES

¾ cup flour
¼ teaspoon salt
4 eggs

1¾ cups milk
2 tablespoons butter, melted
   and cooled

FIRST METHOD

Place all ingredients except butter in electric blender. Blend at high speed until smooth. With blender at low speed, slowly add melted butter, leaving white sediment of butter in bottom of pan. Turn blender to high for 30 seconds.

Set batter aside at room temperature for 1 hour before making crêpes, or refrigerate covered up to 8 hours before making them.

SECOND METHOD

Combine flour, salt, and eggs in mixing bowl. Blend with wire whisk. Add milk and continue beating until batter is smooth. Strain through a fine sieve. Add cooled butter slowly, leaving white sediment of butter at bottom of pan, and blend. Set aside at room temperature for 1 hour before making crêpes, or refrigerate covered up to 8 hours before making them.

TO MAKE CRÊPES

Heat a 5- to 6-inch crêpe pan until a drop of cold water flicked on its surface will evaporate immediately. Using a pastry brush, lightly grease pan with melted butter. Pour in about

2 tablespoons of batter and quickly rotate pan so batter spreads over bottom evenly. Cook crêpe until browned on underside, turn, and cook second side until lightly flecked with brown. Turn out onto plate. Repeat until all batter has been used. Do not stack crêpes while hot. [*Makes* 18 *to* 20 *crêpes.*]

TO STORE

Stack cooled crêpes with wax paper between each, then wrap stack in foil. Refrigerate or freeze until ready to use.

Frozen crêpes will thaw unwrapped at room temperature in 10 to 15 minutes. Reheat in 300° oven a few minutes before filling.

TO SERVE

Spoon about 2 tablespoons of desired filling on each crêpe, fold over, and place in single layer in shallow baking dish. Cover with additional filling or desired sauce. Bake in preheated 350° oven until filling is thoroughly heated, sauce bubbly hot. Serve at once.

Or, heat filling. Spoon onto heated crêpes. Fold over or roll up. Top with additional filling or appropriate sauce. Serve at once.

CRÊPES FOR HORS D'OEUVRES

Spread crêpes with any desired very thick filling, roll up. Cut each crêpe in half if desired. Place seam side down on flat baking sheet. Place in preheated 350° oven until thoroughly heated. Serve at once.

NOTE: Crêpes may be filled and folded or rolled, then frozen until ready to bake. Place not touching on flat tray. Freeze until firm. Pack in aluminum pans. Wrap pans in foil. Store in freezer. Bake frozen in preheated 350° oven. Cover with any well-heated sauce and serve.

SUGGESTED FILLINGS

Creamed chicken, shrimp, lobster, or other seafood; diced or minced cooked beef, veal, pork, lamb in rich thick sauce; diced, cooked vegetables in rich thick cheese sauce.

DESSERT CRÊPES

Add 1 teaspoon sugar, 1 tablespoon cognac, other brandy, Grand Marnier, or kirsch to basic crêpe batter. Proceed as in making basic crêpes.

Dust warm dessert crêpes with confectioners' sugar. Roll up and serve with leftover custard, dessert sauce, or whipped cream.

Fill dessert crêpes with any diced leftover fresh, canned, or stewed fruit mixed with homemade custard sauce (see page 168). Fold over or roll up. Place in single layer in shallow baking pan. Bake at 350° until thoroughly heated. Serve with sweetened whipped cream, ice cream, or any appropriate dessert sauce. (Special touch: add a tablespoon of cognac or any good liqueur to custard sauce.)

Egg Dishes

OMELETS

Almost any small bits and pieces of leftover cooked food can be used to make a filled omelet—from that one piece of crumbled bacon from yesterday's breakfast to that tiny smidgen of overlooked caviar served with cocktails last night.

For the experienced cook there is nothing difficult about preparing a light and fluffy filled omelet. However, this classic way with eggs can be tricky for the novice, so here are two ways to go about it, both equally good.

FILLED OMELET

3 *eggs*
1 *tablespoon water*
Salt ⎱ *to taste*
Pepper ⎰

2 *or* 3 *tablespoons dry filling, such as crumbled crisp-cooked bacon, minced cooked chicken or seafood, finely diced cooked vegetables or meat*

Beat the eggs with the water for about 30 seconds, season with salt and pepper, and stir in the filling.

Grease a 5- to 6-inch omelet pan lightly with butter. Heat to sizzling. Pour in eggs and stir once as you would for scrambled eggs. Cook over high heat, pushing the eggs to the center of the pan as they start to congeal. Do this quickly so that the eggs do not stick. The still-liquid part will flow into the empty spaces, and in about 5 seconds the omelet will be firm but still moist. Fold it over, roll it out onto a warm plate, and serve at once.

[1 *to* 2 *servings.*]

FILLED OMELET WITH SAUCE

Heat ⅓ to ½ cup of moist filling for each 3-egg omelet.

Filling may be creamed chicken or seafood, diced meat in thick gravy or tomato sauce, vegetables in cream or cheese sauce, etc.

Follow basic instructions for filled omelet above but omit filling. As soon as omelet is firm, spoon a little filling onto it, a bit off-center. Fold omelet over and roll out onto warm plate. Spoon remaining hot "filling" over surface and serve at once.

SOUFFLÉS

Nothing is quite as elegant as a light and airy soufflé. Yet, we know of no other dish so easy to prepare that makes such a truly delicious use of leftovers.

3 *tablespoons butter—additional butter to grease soufflé mold*
3 *tablespoons flour*
1 *cup milk*
2 *to 4 tablespoons grated Parmesan or Swiss cheese*

¾ *to 1 cup "filling": finely diced or minced cooked seafood, fowl, or meat, puréed fruit or cooked vegetables*
Salt ⎱ *to taste*
Pepper ⎰
4 *egg yolks, lightly beaten*
5 *egg whites*

Generously butter a 1½- to 2-quart soufflé mold. Refrigerate while preparing soufflé.

Preheat oven to 400°. Melt the butter in a heavy saucepan over moderate heat (do not allow to brown). Stir in the flour and blend well (but again, do not allow to brown). Add the milk, slowly stirring it into the butter-flour mixture as it is added. Continue to stir until sauce is smooth and thick. Remove from heat, add cheese and the desired "filling." Season to taste with salt and pepper, then stir in the beaten egg yolks.

In separate bowl, beat the egg whites with a wire whisk until they will stand in soft peaks when the beater is removed.

Using wire whisk, quickly blend about one-quarter of the beaten egg whites into the sauce mixture. Then gently fold in the remainder with a rubber or wooden spatula. Do not overblend. As soon as egg whites are blended in, pour mixture into prepared mold.

Reduce oven heat to 375°. Place soufflé in the middle of center rack and bake for 25 to 30 minutes or until well puffed and a light golden brown. Serve at once.

[4 *to 6 servings.*]

QUICHE

Though quiche Lorraine is the best-known "quiche," there are many versions of this classic unsweetened custard pie. What's more its possibilities for making use of bits and pieces of cooked food are as numerous as those of soufflés and omelets; to many, the results are twice as delicious.

QUICHE LORRAINE

Unbaked pie pastry for 1 *crust (see page* 220)
¼ *cup diced cooked ham*
¼ *cup diced Gruyère or Swiss cheese*
1 *tablespoon flour*
5 *large or* 6 *small eggs, lightly beaten*

2 *cups light cream*
½ *teaspoon salt*
⅛ *teaspoon freshly ground black pepper*
Dash of grated nutmeg
1 *tablespoon cold butter, cut into thin slices*

Line a 9-inch pie pan with pastry. Refrigerate until chilled.
Combine ham and cheese, dredge with flour. Spread mixture evenly over the bottom of the chilled pastry-lined pie pan.
Combine eggs with cream, salt, pepper, and nutmeg. Blend well and pour over ham and cheese. Dot surface with slivers of butter. Place in a preheated 400° oven and bake for 10 minutes. Reduce heat to 325° and continue to bake until custard has set—about 30 minutes. Serve warm.
[8 *servings as an hors d'oeuvre;* 4 *servings as an entree.*]

CHEDDAR CHEESE AND BACON QUICHE

Substitute crumbled crisp-cooked bacon for ham, soft crumbled cheddar cheese for Gruyère or Swiss.

SEAFOOD QUICHE

Substitute diced cooked shrimp, lobster, crabmeat, or other fish for ham.

VEGETABLE QUICHE

Substitute chopped cooked broccoli, chopped well-drained cooked spinach, or chopped cooked asparagus for ham. Add 1 tablespoon chopped mild sweet onion. Substitute 1 cup sour cream and 1 cup milk for light cream.

CHICKEN QUICHE

Substitute cooked chicken for ham, Greek Feta cheese for Gruyère or Swiss. Add ¼ cup slivered ripe olives.

ANCHOVY-OLIVE QUICHE

Line prepared dough in pie pan with anchovy fillets. Sprinkle slivered ripe olives over fillets. Proceed as in making quiche Lorraine.

MEAT QUICHE WITH SOUR CREAM

Distribute lightly dredged in flour chopped cooked beef, lamb, or pork instead of cheese and ham over prepared dough in pan. Proceed as in making quiche Lorraine. Before baking, combine ¾ cup sour cream with 2 tablespoons grated Parmesan cheese and pour over surface of quiche.

Pastries

FLAKY PASTRY

2 *cups all-purpose flour*
1 *teaspoon salt*
½ *cup shortening*

¼ *cup ice water*
¼ *cup very cold butter, cut into thin slivers*

Sift flour and salt into mixing bowl. Cut in shortening with a pastry blender or two knives until mixture resembles coarse-ground corn meal. Add ice water and blend lightly with a fork. Then, with your hands, quickly form dough into a ball.

Roll out on a lightly floured board or pastry cloth. Sprinkle one-quarter of the butter slivers over surface of half the dough, fold other half over buttered half, and roll out again. Repeat until all butter has been used.

Makes enough dough for one 2-crust 9-inch pie (or two 1-crust 9-inch pies), 12 individual tart shells, or about 24 small filled turnovers.

PÂTÉ À CHOUX

Perhaps the easiest of all the classic French doughs, pâté à choux is certainly one of the most adaptable.

It serves equally well for hot little appetizer beignets or icy cold cream-filled dessert profiteroles. It may also be used to make "light as air" entree-sized pastry shells for creamed chicken or seafood, sauced meat or vegetables.

BASIC CHOUX PASTRY DOUGH

1 *cup water*
½ *cup butter, room tempera-*
ture

½ *teaspoon salt*
1¼ *cups sifted flour*
4 *large or 5 small eggs*

Combine water and butter in saucepan, add salt, and bring
to boil over medium heat. Add the flour all at once and stir
vigorously with a heavy wooden spoon until mixture forms a
stiff dough and leaves the sides of the pan. Remove from heat
and beat in eggs one at a time, beating well after each addition.
When all eggs have been added, continue to beat until dough
is smooth, shiny, and elastic.
[*Makes about* 36 *small beignets.*]

TO MAKE COCKTAIL BEIGNETS

Add ¼ to ½ cup minced lean boiled or baked ham, minced
cooked shrimp or lobster, flaked poached salmon, or grated
cheese to basic chou batter after beating in eggs. Blend well.

Drop dough by spoonfuls (spaced about 2 inches apart)
onto ungreased baking sheet. Bake in a preheated 400° oven
until beignets are well puffed, crisp, shiny, and lightly browned
—about 15 minutes.

Or, drop dough by spoonfuls into hot deep fat and fry until
beignets are puffed and lightly browned.

Serve beignets warm.
[*Makes about* 36 *small beignets.*]

NOTE: Baked or fried beignets may be made ahead and refrigerated
or frozen. Reheat cold or frozen beignets in 350° oven before serving.

CHEESE PUFFS FOR ENTREES

Prepare basic choux dough. Add ½ cup grated cheese after
adding eggs. Fill a pastry bag (one with a No. 6 or 8 plain

tip) three-quarters full with dough. Press out 2- to 2½-inch rounds on ungreased baking sheet. Bake in a preheated 400° oven for 10 minutes. Reduce heat to 350° and bake until puffs are lightly browned (about 20 additional minutes).

Remove from oven and pierce each puff with a sharp knife so that steam may escape. Cool slightly. Cut tops from puffs and fill with any desired hot creamed or sauced cooked food. [*Makes about 36 small puffs.*]

NOTE: Puffs may be made ahead and refrigerated or frozen until ready to use. Reheat in 350° oven.

DESSERT PÂTÉ À CHOUX FOR PROFITEROLES
(*Cream Puffs*)

Add 1 tablespoon sugar to flour before adding to boiling water and butter. Proceed as in preparing basic recipe. Make large or small puffs. Bake or fry as in making beignets or entree puffs.

Cool, split, and fill with leftover sweetened whipped cream, with custard, ice cream, or chopped or diced cooked fruit. Serve with a chocolate, custard, or fruit sauce.

Salad Dressings

MAYONNAISE

Homemade mayonnaise can add such superb flavor to any cold leftovers that it would seem worth the price of an electric blender to make the making easy—even if used for mayonnaise alone. Moreover, the cost would be justified. Blender mayonnaise costs far less than the commercial variety.

BASIC MAYONNAISE

2 *eggs*
2 *tablespoons lemon juice*
¾ *teaspoon salt*
¼ *teaspoon dry mustard*
  (*optional*)

⅛ *teaspoon white pepper*
1 *cup salad oil*

Place all ingredients except ½ cup of the salad oil in an electric blender. Cover and blend at high speed for 15 seconds. Remove cover and add remaining oil in a thin steady stream. Turn off motor as soon as all oil is added.
[*Makes about* 2 *cups mayonnaise.*]

CHIVE MAYONNAISE

Blend 2 tablespoons chopped chives into prepared mayonnaise.

CURRY MAYONNAISE

Add 2 tablespoons curry powder, 1 tablespoon soy sauce to prepared mayonnaise. Blend for 15 seconds in electric blender.

ROQUEFORT MAYONNAISE

Combine ¾ cup crumbled Roquefort cheese with ½ cup sour cream. Mash with fork until smooth. Combine with prepared mayonnaise and blend well.

HERB MAYONNAISE

Add 2 tablespoons chopped chives, 2 tablespoons chopped parsley, 1 teaspoon crushed tarragon, and 1 teaspoon crushed chervil to prepared mayonnaise. Blend.

RUSSIAN DRESSING

Add ¼ cup chili sauce, 2 tablespoons each chopped chives, chopped pimiento, and chopped sweet mixed pickle to mayonnaise. Blend well.

CREAMY FRENCH DRESSING

2 *eggs*	⅛ *teaspoon Beau Monde*
½ *teaspoon salt*	*seasoning*
¼ *teaspoon pepper*	1½ *cups salad oil*
¼ *teaspoon paprika*	¼ *cup red wine vinegar*

Combine eggs, salt, pepper, paprika, and Beau Monde seasoning in electric blender. Cover and blend for 15 seconds. Remove cover and add 1 cup of the oil in a thin steady stream. Add the wine vinegar in the same manner, then add the remaining oil and blend for a final 15 seconds.
[*Makes about* 2 *cups dressing.*]

NOTE: This dressing may be made ahead and used as needed. Refrigerate covered.

VINAIGRETTE, OR FRENCH, DRESSING

Vinaigrette dressing and what we Americans call French dressing are actually one and the same.

The French "dress" a salad at the table by adding oil to the prepared greens. The greens are then well tossed so that they are coated with oil; seasoning is added, the salad is tossed once again, the vinegar is poured on, and the salad is tossed once more.

The American chef, always ready to oversimplify, combines the oil, seasoning, and vinegar and adds it to the greens, which, of course, is easier but rather a sad little mistake. The French method makes a crisper, far more delicious salad.

Nonetheless, no cookbook is complete without a recipe for "French dressing." How you add it to your salad depends on you. As a vinaigrette dressing, it is a marinade, or, if you prefer, a dressing for meats as well as vegetables or greens.

¼ cup vinegar (*white or red wine vinegar, tarragon vinegar, or, if preferred, fresh lemon juice*)
1 teaspoon salt, *or salt, to taste*
¼ teaspoon pepper, *or pepper, to taste (freshly ground black pepper is preferable)*

¼ teaspoon sugar (*optional*)
⅛ to ¼ teaspoon dry mustard (*optional*)
¾ cup oil (*olive oil, peanut oil, or any preferred salad oil*)

Combine vinegar and seasonings, blend with fork or wire whisk. Add oil, beat with wire whisk until blended.
[*Makes about 1 cup dressing.*]

Sample Menus

DINNER FOR NEXT WEEK

ROAST BEEF

Rare Beef Slices with Red Wine Sauce*
Château Potatoes*
Salad
of
Endive and Avocado Slices
Vinaigrette Dressing
French Bread
Chocolate Bread Pudding*

Beef Stroganoff*
with Flat Noodles
French Peas
Cauliflower Salad*
Crusty Hot Rolls
Fresh Pears
poached in
Orange Juice and Kirsch

Roast Beef Hash*
Fried Tomato Slices
Sugar-glazed Boiled Carrots
Baked Apples
with
Whipped Cream Balls*

* Recipes are included in the book. See Index.

POT ROAST

Casserole of Beef with Potatoes*
Green Bean Salad*
Corn Sticks
Stewed Fruit in Port
with
Ice Cream

Jellied Summer Vegetable Soup*
Beef Biscuit Roll*
Fresh Lima Beans   Spiced Beets
Soufflé with Fruit Filling*

ALREADY-READY PARTY MENUS

VEAL

Veal Marengo* with Rice*
Salad of Mixed Greens*
French Bread
Camembert Cheese
Fresh Pears

Veal with Mushrooms Paprika*
Rice and Peas
Fresh Fruit Salad
Apple Pie
with
Peach Ice Cream

TOMORROW NIGHT'S SUPPER

BOILED BEEF

Boiled Beef Slices
with Easy Cranberry-Orange Relish*
Boiled New Potatoes in Jackets
Salad of
Tender Young Spinach Leaves
with Crumbled Bacon
French Dressing
Rye Bread
Fresh Strawberries
with
Vanilla Ice Cream

Boeuf en Gelée*
(Jellied Beef)
Potatoes Chantilly*
Crisp-cooked Vegetable Salad*
Spiced Peaches   Hot Rolls
Celery, Olives, and Radishes
in ice bowl
Fresh Pineapple Slices in Kirsch
Crisp Cookies

ANYTIME DINNERS

CHICKEN, DUCK, TURKEY

Cold Chicken Mayonnaise Collée*
Asparagus Vinaigrette
Peach Halves
broiled with
Sour Cream and Brown Sugar
Hot Baking Powder Biscuits

German Bread Pudding
Whipped Cream

Brandied Duck with Herbs*
Plain Boiled Noodles
Grapefruit and Avocado Salad
French Dressing
Pistachio Ice Cream
with
Melba Sauce (commercially bottled)

Turkey Hash*
Fried Apple Slices   Lima Beans
Watercress and Boston Lettuce Salad
Vanilla Ice Cream
in
Candied Orange Shells*

MONDAY NIGHT DINNERS

LAMB, PORK

Papoutsakia*
(Greek Lamb-stuffed Eggplant)
Beet and Onion Ring Salad
Greek Bread   Butter
Halva
Greek Coffee

Cold Roast Pork Slices
Vegetables au Gratin*
Spiced Crab Apples   Corn Sticks
Poached Plums with Cognac
Thin Slices of Pound Cake
Coffee

LUNCHEON FOR TOMORROW

HAM

Baked Ham in Cream*
Boiled New Potatoes
with
Parsley Butter
Applesauce
Buttered Beaten Biscuits
Compote
of
Fresh Peach and Orange Slices

Potage St. Germain*
Cold Ham Mousse*
Broccoli and Belgian Endive Salad*
Hot Rolls
Crisp Apple Slices
Cream Cheese and Guava Jelly
Crisp Crackers

DOUBLE-QUICK MEALS

CORNED BEEF

Cold Corned Beef Slices
Frozen Horseradish Whipped Cream*
Hot O'Brien Potatoes*
Mustard Pickles   French Bread
Chocolate Ice Cream
and
Orange Sherbet
(Half and Half)

Corned Beef Hash*
Spicy Pears

Buttered Home-style White
Bread
Celery Sticks   Carrot Curls
Individual Fruit Baked Alaskas*

SUPPERS WITH COOKED
RICE FROM LAST WEEK

Black Beans and Rice*
Cold Ham Slices
Pickled Peaches   Tomato Slices
Rye Bread
Crèma Danica   Preserved Whole Figs
Crackers

Chinese Fried Rice*
Egg Rolls (Frozen)
Pork with Sweet-and-Sour Sauce*
Mandarin Oranges
Fortune Cookies
Tea

Curried Rice*
(with Chicken or Seafood)
Curry Condiments
Hot Rolls
Pineapple Slices
Topped with
Lime Sherbet

SALAD LUNCHEON

POTATOES

Continental Potato Salad*
Rye Bread and Butter Sandwiches
Compote
of
Fresh Fruit
Brownies

Insalata di Patate e Aragosta*
Italian Bread
Mexican Convent Sunday Dessert*

Salad Niçoise*
Thin Watercress and
Butter Sandwiches
Port Salut Cheese
Fresh Figs
and
Plums

QUICK LATE SUPPERS

POTATOES

Spanish Omelet*
Tomato Slices Marinated
in Garlicky
French Dressing
Fresh Peaches   Chocolate Cookies

Farmer's Breakfast*
(Ham and Potatoes)
Broiled Fresh Pineapple Slices

Camembert Cheese
French Bread   Black Grapes

TOMORROW NIGHT'S FISH DINNERS

Seafood Timbales*
Boiled Rice with Parsley and Chives
Chutney-broiled Peach Halves
Bel Paese Cheese
French Bread   Pears

Quick Fish Loaf*
Creamed Potatoes*
Broiled Tomato Halves
(sprinkled with minced onion and brown sugar)
Muenster Cheese with Caraway Seeds
French Bread   Pears or Apples

LUNCHEON WITH SOUP AND . . .

Cream of Vegetable Soup*
Ham Sandwiches on Thin Rye Bread
Mixed Pickles   Celery Stalks
Blackberry Bread Pudding*

Cream of Tomato Soup*
Southern Chicken Salad* Sandwich
Cantaloupe, Banana, and
Orange Compote

Hot Borscht*
Vegetable Salad Mold*
Corn Bread
Deep-Dish Peach Pie
with Sour Cream

Index